Jacqueline Lean is a barrister at Landmark Chambers. Her practice encompasses all matters relating to the use and development of land, including landlord and tenant and real property disputes.

A Practical Guide to Mortgage Possession Proceedings

A Practical Guide to Mortgage Possession Proceedings

Jacqueline Lean

Barrister, Gray's Inn

MA (Cantab) LLM

Law Brief Publishing

Published 2022 by Law Brief Publishing, an imprint of Law Brief Publishing Ltd
30 The Parks
Minehead
Somerset
TA24 8BT

www.lawbriefpublishing.com

Paperback: 978-1-913715-97-7

For N, K and A

PREFACE

The nature and jurisprudential foundation of a mortgage has exercised some of the brightest and best legal minds for many years. This book does not seek to enter that debate. Nor does it attempt to provide a comprehensive overview of the various charges which may fall under the broad term 'mortgage'. What it seeks to do is to focus on the issues which may arise in the possession claims most commonly encountered in this jurisdiction: legal mortgages securing loan agreements, as a first legal charge over (in the main) residential property, with a view to providing a practical guide for those involved in a claim for possession of such property.

This book was written after the provisions in Practice Direction 55C (Coronavirus: temporary provision in relation to possession proceedings) largely ceased to apply to new claims. It is to be expected, however, that the cessation of the protections put in place during 2020, and the continued economic fallout from the pandemic, will see an increase in mortgage possession claims going forward. It remains to be see what, if any, measures may be introduced to address the same, and how it may be taken into account by the courts when exercising the various powers discussed in Chapter 9.

Finally, a number of thanks. Firstly, to the team at Law Brief Publishing who identified a potential need for this book, and who gave me the opportunity to write it. Secondly, to my colleagues at Landmark Chambers for their generous sharing of knowledge and experience over the years. Thirdly, to my family for their continued support, with especial thanks to Ross and Robyn for bed and board when Covid struck far from home mid Chapter 7.

The law is stated as at 21 February 2022.

JACQUELINE LEAN
Landmark Chambers
February 2022

TABLE OF CASES

Abbey National Mortgages v Bernard [1996] 71 P. & C.R. 257

Albany Home Loans Ltd v Massey [1997] 2 All E.R. 609

Arkin v Marshall [2020] 1 W.L.R. 3284

Ashe v National Westminster Bank plc [2008] 1 W.L.R. 710

Bank of Credit and Commercial International SA v Aboody [1990] 1 Q.B. 923

Bank of Ireland v Colliers International UK Plc (In Administration) [2013] 2 W.L.R. 895

Barclays Bank Plc v Alcorn [2002] EWCA Civ 817

Bristol & West Building Society v Ellis [1997] 73 P. & C.R. 158

Bristol & West Building Society v Saunders [1997] B.C.C. 83

Britannia Building Society v Earl [1990] 1 W.L.R. 422

Buchler v Talbot [2004] 2 A.C. 298

Castle Phillips Finance Co Ltd v Piddington [1995] 1 F.L.R. 783

Cheltenham & Gloucester Building Society v Grant [1994] 24 H.L.R. 703

Cheltenham & Gloucester Building Society v Krausz [1997] 29 H.L.R. 597

Cheltenham & Gloucester Building Society v Norgan [1996] 1 W.L.R. 343

City of London Building Society v Flegg [1988] A.C. 54

Cityland and Property (Holdings) Ltd v Dabrah [1968] Ch 166

Commercial First Business Ltd v Munday [2015] 1 P. & C.R. 7

Costco Bulk Carrier Co Ltd v Armada Shipping SA [2011] EWHC 216 (Ch)

Deutsche Bank (Suisse) v Khan [2013] EWHC 482 (Comm)

Dhillon v Barclays Bank Plc [2020] EWCA Civ 619

Evans v Cherry Tree Finance Ltd [2008] EWCA Civ 331

First National Bank v Walker [2001] 1 W.L.R. 505

Global 100 Limited v Laleva [2021] EWCA Civ 1835

Green v Southern Pacific Mortgages Ltd [2018] EWCA Civ 854

Habib Bank AG Zurich v Utocroft 2 Limited [2015] EWHC 3481 (Ch)

Habib Bank Ltd v Taylor [1982] 1 W.L.R. 1218

Halifax Building Society v Clark [1973] Ch 307

Helden v Strathmore Ltd [2011] H.L.R. 41

Horlock v Smith [1842] 11 L.J. Ch 157

Horsham Properties Group Ltd v Clark [2009] 1 W.L.R. 1255

Jackson v Ayles [2021] EWHC 995 (Ch)

Jameer v Paratus AMC [2013] H.L.R. 18

Kasler v OTP Jelzalogbank Zrt [2014] Bus. L.R. 664

Khan v Permayer [2001] B.P.I.R. 95

Landmark Mortgages Ltd v Bamrah [2017] EWHC 2041 (QB)

LBI HF v Stanford [2015] EWHC 3131 (Ch)

Lloyds Bank Plc v Waterhouse [1993] 2 F.L.R. 97

McDonald v McDonald [2015] Ch 357

McDonald v McDonald [2017] A.C. 273

Midland Bank Plc v McGrath [1996] EGCS 61

National and Provincial Building Society v Lloyd [1996] 28 H.L.R. 459

O'Brien v Barclays Bank Plc [1994] 1 A.C. 180

Parker v Braithwaite [1952] 2 All E.R. 837

Parker-Tweedale v Dunbar Bank Plc & ors (No 2) [1991] Ch 26

Peabody Donation Fund Governors v Haly [1986] 19 H.L.R. 145

Places for People Homes Ltd v Sharples [2012] Ch 382

Plevin v Paragon Personal Finance Ltd [2014] 1 W.L.R. 4222

Quennell v Maltby [1979] 1 W.L.R. 318

Re Atlantic Computer Systems Plc [1992] Ch 505

Re: Eileen Davies [1997] 1 B.P.I.R. 619

Re Taylor [2007] Ch 50

Republic of India v India Steamship Co [1998] A.C. 878

Ropaigealach v Barclays Bank Plc [2000] Q.B. 263

Royal Bank of Scotland Plc v Etridge (No 2) [2002] 2 A.C. 773

Royal Bank of Scotland Plc v Luwum [2008] EWCA Civ 648

Royal Trust Co of Canada v Markham [1995] 1 W.L.R. 1416

Saunders v Anglia Building Society [1971] 1 A.C. 1004

Seal v Chief Constable of South Wales Police [2007] 1 W.L.R. 1859

Secretary of State for Work and Pensions v Payne & Cooper [2011] 1 W.L.R. 1723

Southern and District Finance Plc v Barnes [1995] 27 H.L.R. 691

Tarn v Turner [1888] 39 Ch.D 456

Taylor v Ellis [1960] Ch 368

Thakker v Northern Rock (Asset Management) Plc [2014] EWHC 2107.

Thompson v Foy [2010] 1 P. & C.R. 16

TSB Bank Plc v Camfield [1995] 1 W.L.R. 430

Whitehead v Household Mortgage Corp Plc [2003] 1 W.L.R. 1173

ABBREVIATIONS

The following are the main abbreviations used in this book. In each chapter, where the context requires it, some of the main abbreviations are set out again for ease of reference.

AJA 1970	Administration of Justice Act 1970
AJA 1973	Administration of Justice Act 1973
CCA 1974	Consumer Credit Act 1974
CPR	Civil Procedure Rules 1998 (as amended)
CRA 2015	Consumer Rights Act 2015
DHR 2010	Dwelling House (Execution of Possession Orders by Mortgagees) Regulations 2010
DRSR 2020	Debt Respite Scheme (Breathing Space Moratorium and Mental Health Crisis Moratorium) (England and Wales) Regulations 2020
FLA 1996	Family Law Act 1996
FSMA 2000	Financial Services and Markets Act 2000
IA 1986	Insolvency Act 1986
LPA 1925	Law of Property Act 1925
LRA 2002	Land Registration Act 2002
MCD 2015	Mortgage Credit Directive Order 2015
MRPTA 2010	Mortgage Repossessions (Protection of Tenants etc) Act 2010
Pre-Action Protocol	Mortgage Arrears Pre-Action Protocol for Possession Claims Based on Mortgage or Home Purchase Plan Arrears in Respect of Residential Property

RAO 2001	Financial Services and Markets Act (Regulated Services) Order 2001
UTCCR 1999	Unfair Terms in Consumer Contracts Regulations 1999

Throughout this book, I have sought to use the terms "mortgagor" and "mortgagee" except where the legislation or guidance uses different terms. Where pronouns are deployed, save where referring to a particular party to a claim (where I have tried to ensure the pronoun reflects the person referred to), I have generally reverted to the masculine singular, in line with the majority of the legislation referred to in this book.

CONTENTS

CHAPTER ONE

MORTGAGES AND THE RIGHT TO POSSESSION: AN OVERVIEW

1.1 In broad terms, the essence of a mortgage transaction is that a charge is taken over property as security for performance of an obligation. In practical terms, that will commonly take the form of a legal charge[1] over property securing a loan which facilitated its purchase, or a legal charge over property securing business lending.

1.2 Historically, a mortgage took the form of a conveyance of the freehold (or leasehold[2]) estate to the mortgagee (the lender), subject to a condition subsequent on a fixed date, the property being reconveyed to the mortgagor (the borrower) on satisfaction of the obligation. That position was altered by the Law of Property Act 1925 (LPA 1925),[3] with the mortgagor retaining legal title to the freehold or leasehold estate, and the legal mortgage created either by a charge by deed expressed to be by way of legal mortgage or, prior to 13 October 2013[4] (i) a demise for a term of years absolute subject to cesser on

---

[1]It is questionable whether an equitable mortgagee has a right to take possession of property, not having any legal estate in the land, at least in the absence of a term in the agreement conferring such a right on the mortgagee, or other provision by which the mortgagee may enjoy such a right.

[2] Or the granting of a sub-lease, one day shorter than the lease, with a proviso that the sub-lease would cease on redemption.

[3] LPA 1925 ss 85(1) and 86(1).

[4] Section 23(1) of the Land Registration Act 2002 (LRA 2002) provides that, in respect of a registered estate, the owner's powers do not include granting a mortgage by demise or sub-demise.

redemption (for a freehold estate)[5] or (ii) a sub-demise for a term of years absolute subject to cesser on redemption, the term being at least one day shorter than the leasehold interest vested in the mortgagor (for leasehold land).[6]

1.3 A charge by way of legal mortgage must be made by deed, be expressed to be by way of legal mortgage[7] (although the exact phrase "charge by way of legal mortgage" does not need to be used[8]) and, for registered land, completed by registration to have effect.[9] A mortgagee pursuant to a legal charge created by deed has the same protections, powers and remedies as if he were a mortgagee by demise or sub-demise. That includes the right to take proceedings to obtain possession from the occupiers and the persons in receipt of rents and profits.[10]

1.4 The mortgagee of a mortgage made by deed also has a number of powers conferred by LPA 1925 s.101 to the same extent as if they had been provided for under the terms of the mortgage deed, but subject to the terms of the mortgage deed and insofar as a contrary intention is not in the same, including:

(i) A power, when the mortgage money has become due, to sell or concur in selling the property;

---

[5] LPA 1925 s. 85(1).

[6] LPA 1925 s.86(1).

[7] LPA 1925 s.87.

[8] See *Cityland and Property (Holdings) Ltd v Dabrah* [1968] Ch 166, and, for registered land, LRA 2002 ss 6 and 7.

[9] LRA 2002 ss 6 and 7. All charges created by means of a registrable disposition take effect as charges created by deed by way of legal mortgage after 13 October 2003 pursuant to LRA 2002 s.51.

[10] LPA 1925 s.87.

(ii) A power to insure the property, with the premiums paid secured under the charge in addition to the mortgage money;

(iii) A power, when the mortgage money has become due, to appoint a receiver of the income of the mortgaged property or any part thereof.

1.5 In principle, the mortgagee has an immediate right to commence an action for possession of the property – subject to any agreement to the contrary. That is, however, subject to a number of qualifications and restrictions.

1.6 Firstly, the mortgage deed itself. The deed (or agreement it gives effect to) will commonly provide that the mortgagee will not exercise his right to seek possession provided that the mortgagor maintains the payments due under the mortgage and/or complies with any other terms or conditions of the mortgage agreement.[11] If seeking possession in such a case the mortgagee will need to demonstrate that the conditions for seeking possession in the event of the default relied on have been met, and that any notices or other procedures provided for under the agreement have been strictly complied with.

1.7 Secondly, where a mortgage secures a regulated mortgage contract or a regulated agreement under the Consumer Credit Act 1974 (CCA 1974),[12] the right to possession is only enforceable pursuant to an order of the court.[13]

[11] Such a restriction *might* be implied into a mortgage agreement (if, for example, if provides for monies to be payable in instalments) – although the court is not likely to take such a course lightly.

[12] See Chapter 2.

[13] CCA 1974 s.126 provides that a land mortgage securing (a) a regulated agreement, (b) a regulated mortgage contract, or (c) a consumer credit agreement which would, but for article 60D of the Financial Services and Markets Act 2000 (Regulated Activities) Order 2001, is enforceable on order of the court only.

1.8 Thirdly, if a receiver has already been appointed by the court in respect of the property at the request of a third party,[14] the mortgagee cannot enter into possession of the property unless his right to do so was expressly reserved in the order appointing the receiver. If that is the case, the mortgagee will either need to apply to court for the receiver to be discharged, or for leave to bring an action for recovery of the land.

1.9 Fourthly, if a claim to an overriding interest is made by an occupier of the property.[15]

1.10 Fifthly, if a claim is brought against one joint-mortgagor and the other is in possession and has an arguable defence. For example, in *Albany Home Loans Ltd v Massey* [1997] 2 All E.R. 609 the mortgagee (Albany Home Loans Ltd) sought possession of a property jointly owned by a husband and wife who were also joint mortgagors. An order for possession was made against the husband, the trial judge having dismissed his defence that the arrears had arisen because he had been wrongfully dismissed from the claimant company. A possession order had not been made as against the wife, as her defence, based on undue influence, were awaiting trial. The Court of Appeal made clear that where the ejection of one of two mortgagors was of no benefit to the mortgagee (the making of the possession order at that time not being necessary to protect the rights of the mortgagee) it was *"not in general right to make an order requiring him to leave within the period during which the other mortgagee is in possession and entitled to be in possession".*[16] That was

[14] See para 1.13 below.

[15] See Schedule 3 to the LRA 2002 and Chapter 6.

[16] Per Schiemann L.J at pg 613. In a Coda to his judgment, Schiemenn L.J. also provided some practical guidance on the 'appropriate course' to be followed where a district judge was faced with a submission by one mortgagor that an order for possession against him would not advantage the mortgagee because another mortgagor was entitled to remain in possession. *"In general such a submission will have force. There are no doubt a number of ways in which effect could be given to it. It seems to me that the judge in those circumstances, in the absence of an undertaking on the lines of the one in the*

particularly the case where the two mortgagors shared the home as husband and wife,[17] with reference being made in the judgment to Article 8 of the European Convention of Human Rights[18] and the consequences that could in theory follow if the husband remained in occupation of the property in breach of the court order, or left and subsequently returned to the property whilst his wife remained in occupation.

1.11 Finally, there is also the court's discretion to grant a stay in proceedings relating to residential property under section 36 of the Administration of Justice Act 1970. This is discussed further in Chapter 9.

1.12 Whilst this book is primarily concerned with claims for possession of property – i.e. for the giving up of possession of the property to the mortgagee – it is also important to bear in mind that a mortgagee can enter into possession of property without taking the keys to the property. The mortgagee may, for example, exercise his right of possession by giving notice to the mortgagor's tenants to pay rent directly to him.[19]

1.13 A mortgagee who enters into possession of mortgaged property is, however, subject to a number of duties and liabilities, to the mortgagor and to others who may have an interest in the equity of redemption (for example, other chargees). Where the mortgagee does not seek to sell the property, or to divert the rents of profits to discharge monies due to him under the mortgage, it may therefore be preferable to appoint a receiver in respect of the property: either under the terms of the mortgage agreement or by way of application to the court pursuant to LPA s.101. A receiver appointed under s.101 is considered an

---

present case, ought to adjourn the proceedings with liberty to restore if the other mortgagor leaves the property or an order for possession is made against that mortgagor."

[17] Per Schiemann L.J. at pg 613.

[18] Although the case pre-dated the Human Rights Act 1998.

[19] See, for example, *Horlock v Smith* (1842) 11 L.J. Ch 157.

agent of the mortgagor rather than the mortgagee (even though appointed on application by the mortgagee). However, a receiver appointed under the mortgage deed will be regarded as an agent of the mortgagee unless the mortgage deed provides to the contrary. It is therefore common to find a proviso in the mortgage deed that a receiver will be the agent of the mortgagor.

1.14 A receiver appointed under a mortgage agreement may bring a claim for possession of the property from those in occupation if that falls within the powers conferred on them under the mortgage deed. For example, in *McDonald v McDonald* [2015] Ch 357, the Court of Appeal held that it was open to receivers appointed under a mortgage agreement to serve a notice under s.21 of the Housing Act 1988 terminating an assured shorthold tenancy entered into in breach of the mortgage conditions in their own names (and not in the name of the landlords), the power to serve such notice being reasonably incidental to exercise of the power to sell the property and to take possession of it under the mortgage agreement. Although in *McDonald* the claim for possession was brought in the name of the landlords, it is common to see claims for possession brought by the named receiver(s) acting as receivers / LPA receivers of the mortgagor.

1.15 The position with regards to authorised, and unauthorised tenants of the mortgagor is considered in more detail in Chapter 6.

CHAPTER TWO

STATUTORY REGULATION

2.1 The statutory framework of mortgages is, unfortunately, a rather complicated area, but one which must be at least briefly traversed in order to understand the restrictions which may apply, or defences which may be available, where possession is sought of mortgaged property.[20]

2.2 The Mortgage Arrears Pre-Action Protocol for Possession Claims Based on Mortgage or Home Purchase Plan Arrears in Respect of Residential Property (discussed in more detail in Chapter 4) which applies to certain residential properties, distinguishes between:

(i) First charge residential mortgages and home purchase plans[21] regulated by the Financial Services Authority under the Financial Services and Markets Act 2000 (as amended by the Financial Services Act 2012);

(ii) Second charge mortgages over residential property and other secured loans regulated under the Consumer Credit Act 1974 on residential property; and

(iii) Unregulated residential mortgages.[22]

---

[20] On defences generally, see Chapter 5.

[21] Defined in para 1.1(b) of the Pre-Action Protocol as "a method of purchasing a property by way of a sale and lease arrangement that does not require the payment of interest". A property purchased using a Sharia compliant mortgage arrangement involving the purchase of the property by the 'lender' and a lease of the property to the person who sought its purchase (Ijarah, and Ijarah with diminishing Musharaka) is likely to fall under this definition.

[22] Essentially, a mortgage which is not regulated under the FSMA 2000, CCA 1974 or MCD 2015.

2.3 Whilst those terms are not defined (save for home purchase plans) that framework provides useful starting point, at least in respect of residential property, although it does not capture all of the situations which may arise under the statutory regime.

2.4 The complexity essentially arises due to the interface of mortgages with:

(i) the Financial Services and Markets Act 2000 (FSMA 2000), with its provisions as to "regulated activities" which may only be provided by persons authorised by the Financial Conduct Authority;

(ii) the Financial Services and Markets Act 2000 (Regulated Activities) Order 2001 (RAO 2001) which specifies the activities falling under the auspices of the 2000 Act;

(iii) the Mortgage Credit Directive Order 2015 (MDC 2015) which effectively brought most residential mortgages under the auspices of the FSMA 2000, removing them from the Consumer Credit Act 1974 regime; and

(iv) the Consumer Credit Act 1974 (CCA 1974).

A detailed analysis of the various instruments and changes over the years is outside the scope of this book, but a broad overview is provided below.

The Financial Services and Markets Act 2000 & Regulated Activities Order

2.5 Pursuant to FSMA 2000 s.22(1), an activity is a "regulated activity" for the purposes of the Act if:

"... it is an activity of a specified kind carried on by way of business and

(a) relates to an investment of a specified kind; or

(b) in the case of an activity of a kind which is also specified for the purposes of this paragraph, is carried on in relation to property of any kind."

2.6 No person may carry on a regulated activity in the UK unless he is either an "authorised person" or an "exempt person".[23] This is referred to as the "general prohibition".[24] An agreement made by a person in the course of carrying out a regulated activity in breach of the general prohibition is unenforceable against the other party,[25] save with the permission of the Court.[26] The innocent party is entitled to recover any money or other property paid or transferred by him under the agreement (and compensation for any loss sustained by him as a result of having paid it)[27] but if he elects to do so, he must repay any money and return any other property received by him under the agreement.[28].

2.7 RAO 2001 Article 61 provides that both entering into, and administering, a "regulated mortgage contract" (subject to certain qualifications) is a specified kind of activity for the purposes of s.22 FSMA 2000.

2.8 As originally enacted (and in force from 31 October 2004), Article 61 defined a "regulated mortgage contract" as a contract under which –

---

[23] FSMA 2000 s.19(2). "Authorised person" is defined in s.31. An "exempt person" means a person who is exempt from the general prohibition in relation to that activity as a result of an exemption order made under s.38(1) or as a result of ss39(1) or 285: see 417.

[24] FSMA 2000 s.19 (1).

[25] FSMA 2000 s.27(1).

[26] FSMA s.28(3).

[27] FSMA 2000 s.27.

[28] FSMA 2000 s.28(7).

"(i) a person ("the lender") provides credit to an individual or to trustees ("the borrower"); and

(ii) the obligation of the borrower to repay is secured by a first legal mortgage on land (other than timeshare accommodation) in the United Kingdom, at least 40% of which is used, or is intended to be used, as or in connection with a dwelling by the borrower or (in the case of credit provided to trustees) by an individual who is a beneficiary of the trust, or by a related person."[29]

2.9 Article 61 has been amended on a number of occasions since it was enacted, including:

(i) excluding a "regulated home purchase plan"[30] from the definition of "regulated mortgage contract" (with effect from 6 November 2006);

(ii) the inclusion of properties within the European Economic Area within the definition of "regulated mortgage contract" with effect from 20 April 2015;

---

[29] Article 61(3)(a). "Related person" was defined in Article 61(4)(c) as meaning (in relation to the borrower or to the beneficiary under a trust where credit was provided to trustees) that person's spouse; a person (whether or not of the opposite sex) whose relationship with that person had the characteristics of the relationship between husband and wife; or that person's parent, brother, sister, child, grandparent or grandchild. It was amended in 2005 to include civil partners.

[30] Defined in Article 63F(3). In essence, a regulated home purchase plan is an agreement by which the "home purchase provider" (in effect, the lender) purchases an interest, or undivided share of an interest, in a property, the arrangement provides for the "home purchaser" (in effect, the borrower) to buy out that interest at the end of a qualifying period, and the home purchaser, beneficiary under a trust (if purchased by trustees) or related person is entitled to occupy at least 40% of the property as or in connection with a dwelling and intends to do so.

(iii) the introduction of further, specified, exemptions to the definition, included in a new Article 61A with effect from 5 November 2015; and

(iv) the inclusion of contracts entered into after 31 October 2004 which were 'regulated credit agreements'[31] immediately before 21 March 2016, within the categories of contracts whose administration was a specified kind of activity for the purposes of FSMA 2000 s.22(1).

2.10 Importantly, the qualification that the obligation to repay be secured as a first legal mortgage was removed with effect from 20 March 2016, and, as stated above, the MCD 2015 effectively brought all residential mortgages within the FSMA 2000 regime, with the definition of "regulated agreement" in CCA 1974 s.8 being amended to exclude all mortgages covered by the Mortgage Credit Directive.[32]

2.11 Article 61 currently provides as follows:

"(1) Entering into a regulated mortgage contract as lender is a specified kind of activity.

(2) Administering a regulated mortgage contract is also a specified kind of activity, where—

(a) the contract was entered into by way of business[33] on or after 31st October 2004; or

[31] Defined in RAO 2001 Article 60B.

[32] Directive 2014/17/EU of the European Parliament and of the Council of 4 February 2014 on credit agreements for consumers relating to residential immovable property.

[33] This term is not defined in the RAO 2001, so if there is a dispute in any given case, this will be question of judgment for the court. For a list of factors which the court is likely to consider, there is helpful guidance in *Helden v Strathmore Ltd* [2010] EWHC 2012 (Ch) paras 40-41, not doubted by the CA on appeal [2011] H.L.R. 41, and

(b) the contract—

(i) was entered into by way of business before 31st October 2004, and

(ii) was a regulated credit agreement immediately before 21st March 2016.

(3) In this Chapter—

(a) subject to paragraph (5), a contract is a "regulated mortgage contract" if, at the time it is entered into, the following conditions are met—

(i) the contract is one under which a person ("the lender") provides credit to an individual or to trustees ("the borrower");

(ii) the contract provides for the obligation of the borrower to repay to be secured by a mortgage on land;

(iii) at least 40% of that land is used, or is intended to be used—

(aa) in the case of credit provided to an individual, as or in connection with a dwelling; or

(bb) in the case of credit provided to a trustee which is not an individual, as or in connection with a dwelling by an

---

Jackson v Ayles [2021] EWHC 995 (Ch). In the latter case, the Judge (Chief ICC Judge Briggs) referred to guidance from FCA that the "by way of business" test could be satisfied by an activity undertaken on an isolated occasion, and made clear that lending did not need to be the sole purpose of the individual's business and could form only a small part of the same.

individual who is a beneficiary of the trust, or by a related person;

but such a contract is not a regulated mortgage contract if it falls within article 61A(1) or (2);

(b) "administering" a regulated mortgage contract means either or both of—

(i) notifying the borrower of changes in interest rates or payments due under the contract, or of other matters of which the contract requires him to be notified; and

(ii) taking any necessary steps for the purposes of collecting or recovering payments due under the contract from the borrower;

but a person is not to be treated as administering a regulated mortgage contract merely because he has, or exercises, a right to take action for the purposes of enforcing the contract (or to require that such action is or is not taken);

(c) "credit" includes a cash loan, and any other form of financial accommodation.

(4) For the purposes of paragraph 3(a)—

(a) "mortgage" includes a charge and (in Scotland) a heritable security;

(aa) "land"—

(i) in relation to a contract entered into before IP completion day[34], means land in the United

[34] i.e. 31 December 2020.

Kingdom or within the territory of an EEA State;

(ii) in relation to a contract entered into on or after IP completion day, means land in the United Kingdom.

(b) the area of any land which comprises a building or other structure containing two or more storeys is to be taken to be the aggregate of the floor areas of each of those storeys;

(c) "related person", in relation to the borrower or (in the case of credit provided to trustees) a beneficiary of the trust, means—

(i) that person's spouse or civil partner;

(ii) a person (whether or not of the opposite sex) whose relationship with that person has the characteristics of the relationship between husband and wife; or

(iii) that person's parent, brother, sister, child, grandparent or grandchild;

(5) In this Chapter, a contract entered into before 21st March 2016 is a "regulated mortgage contract" only if—

(a) at the time it was entered into, entering into the contract was an activity of the kind specified by paragraph (1), or

(b) the contract is a consumer credit back book mortgage contract within the meaning of article 2 of the Mortgage Credit Directive Order 2015."

2.12 There is now no requirement for the property to be used, or intended for use, as a dwelling by the borrower in order to constitute a regulated mortgage contract under Article 61: see Article 61(3).

2.13 As set out in Article 61(3), a mortgage is not a "regulated mortgage contract" if the exemptions in Article 61A(1) or (2) apply. The types of agreement specified in Article 61A (1) are:

(a) A regulated home purchase plan;[35]

(b) A limited payment second charge bridging loan;[36]

(c) A second charge business loan;[37]

(d) An investment property loan;[38]

(e) An exempt consumer buy-to-let mortgage contract;[39]

---

[35] See Article 63F and fn21 above.

[36] An agreement financing the purchase of land, used by the borrower as a temporary financing solution whilst transitioning to another finance arrangement, where the mortgage ranks in priority behind one or more other mortgages affecting the land in question and no more than 4 payments are to be made by the borrower under the agreement (see Article 61A(6)).

[37] A contract that at the time entered into meets the conditions in Article 61(3)(a)(i) – (iii); the lender provides the borrower with credit exceeding £25,000; the mortgage ranks in priority behind one or more other mortgages of the land; and the agreement is entered into by the borrower wholly or predominantly for the purposes of a business carried on, or intended to be carried on, by the borrower (see Article 61A(6)).

[38] A contract that at the time it is entered into meets the conditions in Article 61(3)(a)(i)-(iii); with less than 40% of the land subject to the mortgage used or intended to be used as a dwelling by the borrower, an individual who is a beneficiary of a trust or related person; and the agreement is entered into by the borrower wholly or predominantly for the purposes of a business carried on, or intended to be carried on, by the borrower (Article 61A(6)).

[39] A contract that at the time it is entered into is a consumer buy-to-let mortgage contract within the meaning of Article 4 of the MCD 2015, and is either an agreement to which s.423A(3) FSMA 2000 applies or is a bridging loan (Article 61A(6)).

(f) An exempt equitable mortgage bridging loan;[40] or

(g) An exempt housing authority loan.[41]

2.14 A contract falls under Article 61A(2) if:

(a) It is a limited interest second charge credit union loan;[42]

(b) The borrower receives timely information on the main features, risks and costs of the contract at the pre-contractual stage; and

(c) Any advertising is fair, clear and not misleading.

The Consumer Credit Act 1974

2.15 Mortgage regulation under the FSMA 2000 began on 31 October 2004. Mortgages entered into before that date were, until 21 March 2016, regulated under the CCA 1974 provided they did not exceed the applicable financial thresholds at the date they were entered into. Those thresholds were:

(i) £5,000, before 20 May 1985;

[40] A bridging loan which is secured by an equitable mortgage on land, and is an exempt agreement within the meaning of Article 60B(3) (regulated credit agreements) by virtue of article 60E(2) (exempt agreements: exemptions relating to the nature of the lender) (Article 61A(6)).

[41] A contract that provides for credit to be granted by a housing authority within the meaning of Article 60E which, if entered into on or after 21 March 2016 (i) is an agreement to which s.423A(3) FSMA 2000 applies, (ii) is a bridging loan, or (iii) is a restricted public loan within the meaning of Article 60HA in respect of which the borrower receives timely information on the main features, risks and costs at the pre-contractual stage, and any advertising is fair, clear and not misleading (Article 61A(6)).

[42] Essentially, a borrower-lender agreement where the lender is a credit union, the mortgage ranks in priority behind another mortgage/s of the property and the rate of the total charge for credit does not exceed 42.6% (Article 61A(6)).

(ii) £15,000 between 20 May 1985 and 30 April 1998; and

(iii) £25,000 between 1 May 1998 and 31 October 2004

2.16 From 21 March 2016, first charge mortgages entered into prior to 31 October 2004 which were previously regulated as consumer credit agreements under the CCA 1974 became regulated mortgage contracts under FSMA 2000.[43]

2.17 As currently in force, CCA 1974 s.8(3) provides that a consumer credit agreement[44] is a regulated credit agreement for the purposes of the Act if:

"(a) it is a regulated credit agreement for the purposes of Chapter 14A of Part 2 of the [ROA 2001]; and

(a) if entered into on or after 21 March 2016 it is not an agreement the purpose of which is the acquisition or retention, by an individual acting for purposes outside those of any trade, business or profession carried on by the individual of property rights in land or in an existing or projected building."

2.18 A "regulated credit agreement" for the purposes of Chapter 14A of Part 2 ROA 2001 is defined in ROA 2001 Article 60B:

"(a) in the case of an agreement entered into on or after 21 April 2014, any credit agreement which is not an exempt agreement; or

---

[43] Pursuant to the amendments made by the Financial Services and Markets Act 2000 (Regulated Activities) (Amendment) Order 2016.

[44] A consumer credit agreement is defined in CCA 1974 s.8(1) in very similar terms to a "credit agreement" under the RAO 2001 Article 60B(3): it is a personal credit agreement (i.e. between an individual and any other person) by which that person provides the individual with credit

(b) in the case of an agreement entered into before 21 April 2014, a credit agreement which –

(i) was a regulated agreement within the meaning of section 189(1) of the Consumer Credit Act 1974 when the agreement was entered into; or

(ii) became such a regulated agreement after being varied or supplemented by another agreement before 1st April 2014,

and would not be an exempt agreement pursuant to article 60C(2) on 21 March 2016 if the agreement were entered into on that date."

2.19 A "credit agreement" is an agreement between an individual and any other person by which the credit of any amount is provided to the individual by the other person.[45] An "exempt agreement" means an agreement falling within RAO 2001 Articles 60C – 60H.[46] In broad terms:

(i) A regulated mortgage contract or regulated home purchase plan;[47]

(ii) A loan of £25,000 where the borrower entered into the agreement wholly or predominantly for the purpose for the purpose of a business being carried on, or intended to be carried on, by the borrower;[48]

(iii) Certain loans of less than £25,000, where the borrower entered into the agreement wholly or predominantly for

---

[45] Article 60B(3)

[46] Article 60B(3)

[47] Article 60C

[48] Article 60C(3)

the purpose for the purpose of a business being carried on, or intended to be carried on, by the borrower;[49]

(iv) Loans secured against land where less than 40% of the property is used, or intended to be used, in connection with a dwelling by the borrower or related person of the borrower or, in the case of credit provided to trustees, by an individual who is a beneficiary of the trust or related person of that individual;[50]

(v) A loan where the lender is a local authority or other specified person[51];

(vi) A loan where limited numbers of repayments are to be made;[52]

(vii) Loans made, or entered into, by specified categories of parties and where the charge for credit or interest charge is restricted;[53]

(viii) Loans entered into by an individual with earnings and/or assets above specified thresholds, where the agreement includes a declaration that the borrower agrees to forego the protection and remedies that would be available to the borrower if the agreement were a regulated credit agreement, and which complies with the rules made by the FCA for that purpose; a statement has been made as to the borrower's income or assets which complies with any rules made by the FCA for that purpose; the connection between the statement

[49] Article 60C(4), (4A)

[50] Article 60D, subject to the exceptions in Article 60D(4).

[51] Article 60E.

[52] Article 60F

[53] For details, see Article 60G

and agreement complies with any rules made by the FCA for that purpose; and the statement has been provided to the lender before the agreement was entered into.[54]

2.20 In terms of the position prior to 21 April 2014, the question of whether a particular contract was a regulated agreement under s.8(3) CCA 1974 and was not an exempt agreement falling within CCA 1974 s.16, 16A or s.16B as in force at the date of the agreement (as entered into or a supplemented or varied) will require careful consideration of those provisions as they stood at the date in question, provided always that they would not have been an exempt agreement under Article 60C RAO 2001 if entered into on 21 March 2016.[55]

Buy-to-let mortgages

2.21 Since 21 March 2016, certain buy-to-let mortgages have fallen under the FSMA 2000 regime, as a result of amendments made to ROA 2001 Article 61 by the MCD 2015.

2.22 A "buy-to-let mortgage contract" is defined in MCD 2015 Article 4 as a contract that:

"(a) at the time it is entered into –

(i) meets the conditions in paragraphs (i) to (iii) of article 61(3)(a) [RAO 2001] (regulated mortgage contracts); and

(ii) provides that the land subject to the mortgage cannot at any time be occupied as a dwelling by the borrower or by a related person,[56] and is to be

[54] Article 60H.

[55] i.e. a regulated mortgage contract or regulated home purchase plan.

[56] Which has the same meaning of the term as defined in RAO 2001 Article 61A.

occupied as a dwelling on the basis of a rental agreement; or

(b) is a regulated credit agreement within the meaning of article 60B of the [RAO 2001][57] which –

(i) falls within Article 3(1)(b) of the mortgages directive;[58] and

(ii) provides that the land, or existing or projected building, to which it relates cannot at any time be occupied as a dwelling by the borrower or related person, and is to be occupied as a dwelling on the basis of a rental agreement."[59]

2.23 A "consumer buy-to-let mortgage contract" is a buy-to-let contract which is not entered into by the borrower wholly or predominantly for the purpose of a business carried on or intended to be carried on by the borrower.[60]

2.24 Part 3 of the MCD 2015 introduces a new, bespoke, regulatory regime for consumer buy-to-let mortgages. Buy-to-let mortgages which are entered into for business purposes do not fall within Part 3.

---

[57] See para 2.18 above.

[58] Directive 2014/17/EU of the European Parliament and of the Council of 4 February 2014 on credit agreements for consumers relating to residential immovable property and amending Directives 2008/48/EC and 2013/36/EU and Regulation (EU) No 1093/2010. Article 3(1)(b) relates to "credit agreements the purpose of which is to acquire or retain property rights in land or in an existing or projected building".

[59] If the agreement does not provide that the property is not to be occupied by the borrower or related person, the contract may constitute a regulated mortgage contract, if the property will also be occupied by the borrower, and provided the conditions in RAO 2001 Article 61 are met.

[60] MCD 2015 Article 4(1).

Relevance

2.25 Where a contract is a regulated mortgage contract, the powers under Part 9 CCA 1974 are available to the court, except for that under s.140B CCA 1974.[61] Similarly, where an agreement is a regulated agreement under s.8 CCA 1974, the provisions of Part 9 apply – including s.140B (unfair relationships between creditors and debtors).[62] This is discussed further in Chapters 5 and 9.

61 CCA 1974 s.126(2).

62 CCA 1974 s.126.

CHAPTER THREE

PROCEDURE

Commencing the claim

3.1 A claim for possession of a property brought by (or on behalf of[63]) a mortgagee falls under Part 55 of the CPR.[64] The claim should usually be commenced in the County Court – and must be commenced there if it raises issues where the County Court has exclusive jurisdiction.[65]

3.2 Although there is no longer a requirement that the claim be started at the court in which the property is situated – if the claim is filed at a hearing centre which does not serve the property's address, the claim will be sent to the hearing centre serving that address when it is issued[66] – it is advisable to do so, given the delay which may be involved if the need for transfer arises.

3.3 This provision – and the previous requirement that a claim be started in the County Court for the area where the property was located – can cause some complications where borrowing is secured against more than one property.[67] Whilst possession can

[63] A claim may, for example, be brought by a receiver.

[64] By CPR r.55.2(1)(a) the procedure in Part 55 must be used where a claim includes a possession claim brought by a mortgagee. For the purposes of CPR Part 55 "mortgage" includes a legal or equitable mortgage or legal or equitable charge, and "mortgagee" is to be construed accordingly: r.55.1(c).

[65] Regulated mortgages under the Consumer Credit Act 1974 (CCA 1974 s.141(1)); dwelling houses outside of Greater London which do not include a claim for sale or foreclosure (County Courts Act 1984 s.21(3) & (4)).

[66] CPR r.55.3(1). See further Practice Direction 55A, para 55.3.

[67] For example, where the agreement secured by the mortgage contains an "all monies" clause.

be sought of more than one property in a single claim,[68] if the properties are located in areas served by different hearing centres, experience suggests this may cause some difficulties when seeking to issue the claim in one hearing centre (even if that is the hearing centre serving the majority of the addresses). In practice, this may most conveniently be resolved by issuing a claim in each of the hearing centres in respect of the property (or properties) falling within that centre's area, with an application (or applications) for the claims to be transferred to a single hearing centre and joined for determination. [69]

3.4 A claim for possession by a mortgagee against a mortgagor solely on the grounds of default of payments due under the mortgage may be started using Possession Claims Online provided that (i) it does not include a claim for any other remedy other than possession of the property and payment of money due under the mortgage, interest and costs; (ii) the claimant has an address for service in the UK; (iii) the defendant has an address for service in England or Wales; and (iv) the claimant is able to provide a postcode for the property.[70]

3.5 Possession claims should only be commenced in the High Court if justified by "exceptional circumstances".[71] Practice Direction 55A sets out three sets of circumstances which may, in an appropriate case, justify starting a claim in the High Court including (i) complicated disputes of fact and (ii) points of law of general importance[72] and advises that whilst the value of the

---

[68] Practice Direction 55 notes that by CPR r.7.3 a claimant may use a single claim form to start all claims which can be conveniently disposed of in the same proceedings.

[69] Assuming that there are not "exceptional circumstances" which might justify commencing a claim in the High Court – see para 3.5 below.

[70] Practice Direction 55B para 5.1.

[71] Practice Direction 55A, para 1.1 (1). High Court claims involving a mortgage will be assigned to the Chancery Division: Practice Direction 55A, para 1.6.

[72] Practice Direction 55A para 1.3. Point (3) concerns proceedings against trespassers.

property and amount of any financial claim might be relevant, those factors alone will not normally justify starting the claim in the High Court.[73] If the claim is started in the High Court, the claimant must file a certificate stating the reasons for bringing the claim in the High Court verified by a statement of truth.[74]

3.6 If the claim relates to residential property, and possession is sought on the grounds of arrears, the claimant must first comply with the Mortgage Arrears Pre-Action Protocol for Possession Claims Based on Mortgage or Home Purchase Plan Arrears in Respect of Residential Property[75] ("the Pre-Action Protocol") and two copies of the completed Mortgage pre-action protocol checklist (Form N123) must be brought to the hearing.[76] This is discussed further in Chapter 4.

3.7 The claim should be issued using claim form N5, and, for residential premises, form N120 (Particulars of Claim for possession (mortgaged residential premises)).[77] The particulars of claim must,[78] in any case:

---

[73] Practice Direction 55A para 1.4. Para 2.6 of Practice Direction 29 indicates, more generally, that claims suitable for trial in the High Court include fraud or undue influence claims, and thus where fraud or undue influence is raised as a defence (see Chapter 5) that might provide grounds for a transfer of a claim started in the County Court to the High Court.

[74] CPR r.55.3(2).

[75] Available on the Ministry of Justice website (https://www.justice.gov.uk/courts/procedure-rules/civil/protocol/prot_mha) at date of writing.

[76] Practice Direction 55A, para 5.5.

[77] Practice Direction 55A, para 1.3 read with Practice Direction 4. The prescribed forms are available on the GOV.UK website under the 'County Court Forms' link (https://www.gov.uk/government/collections/county-court-forms) at the time of writing.

[78] Practice Direction 55A, paras 2.1 and 2.5.

(i) Identify the land to which the claim relates;

(ii) State whether the claim relates to residential property;

(iii) State the ground on which possession is claimed. (Whilst the most common ground is likely to be arrears under the mortgage, Form N120 includes a free text box which can be used to provide details of any other basis on which possession is sought);

(iv) Give full details about any mortgage;

(v) Give details of every person who, to the best of the claimant's knowledge, is in possession of the property. (Section 10 of Form N120 requires the claimant to specify whether any tenancy agreement between the borrower and the occupier, or occupiers, named in section 3 (persons known to be in possession of the property) was entered into with or without the authorisation of the mortgagee and, if it was authorised, to explain what steps the mortgagee intends should be taken in respect of that tenancy)[79];

(vi) Set out the state of the mortgage account, including:

- The amount of the advance, any periodic repayment, and any payment of interest required to be paid;

- The amount which would have to be paid (after taking into account any adjustment for early settlement) in order to redeem the mortgage at a stated date not more than 14 days after the claim started, specifying the amount of solicitor's costs and administration charges that would be payable;

[79] The position with regard to third party occupiers is discussed in more detail in Chapter 6.

- The rate of interest payable at the commencement of the mortgage; immediately before the specified arrears accrued; and at the commencement of proceedings.

(vii) If the claim is brought because of the failure to pay periodic payments when due:

- Set out in schedule form the dates and amounts of all payments due and all payments made for a period of two years immediately preceding the date of issue, or from the first date of default if it occurred less than two years before the date of issue, together with a running total of the arrears.[80] If the claimant wishes to rely on a history of arrears that is longer than two years, then these should be set out in a schedule annexed to a witness statement.[81]

- Give details of:

  - Any other payments required to be made as a term of the mortgage (e.g. insurance premiums, administrative charges);

  - Any other sums claimed, stating the nature and amount of each charge; and

  - Whether any of those payments is in arrears and whether or not it is included in the amount of any periodic payment.

(viii) Identify whether or not the loan secured by the mortgage is a regulated consumer credit agreement[82] and, if it is,

[80] Practice Direction 55 para 2.3(2).

[81] Practice Direction 55 para 2.5A.

[82] i.e. an agreement which falls under the CCA 1974 regime.

specify the date on which any notice required by sections 76 or 87 of the Consumer Credit Act 1974 was given;

(ix) If appropriate, details that show the property is not one to which section 141 of the Consumer Credit Act 1974 applies (i.e. that it is not a claim in respect of which the County Court has exclusive jurisdiction);

(x) Set out any relevant information about the defendant's circumstances. In particular:

- Whether the defendant is in receipt of social security benefits;
- Whether any payments are made on his behalf directly to the claimant under the Social Security Contributions and Benefits Act 1992.

(xi) Give details of any tenancy entered into between the mortgagor and mortgagee (including any notices served);

(xii) State any previous steps which the claimant has taken to recover the money secured by the mortgage or the mortgaged property and, in the case of court proceedings, state:

- The dates on which the claim was started and concluded; and
- The dates and terms of any Orders made.

(xiii) If a residential property state whether:

- A Class F land charge has been registered under section 2(7) of the Matrimonial Homes Act 1967;
- A notice registered under section 2(8) or 8(3) of the Matrimonial Homes Act 1983 has been entered and on whose behalf;

- A notice under section 13(10) of the Family Law Act 1996 has been registered and on whose behalf; and

- If so, that the claimant will serve notice of the claim on the persons on whose behalf the land charge is registered or the notice or caution entered.

3.8 It is not normally necessary to claim interest and costs,[83] as there will usually be a contractual entitlement to the same under the terms of the mortgage, but it is always advisable to check the agreement to ensure that that is the case, especially as to whether it provides for costs on an indemnity basis.[84]

3.9 The claim form and particulars of claim must be served on the defendant(s) not less than 21 days before the hearing, together with the prescribed defence form. The claim and supporting documents will usually be served by the court, but if served by the claimant, a certificate of service must be filed prior to the hearing.[85] Where the claim relates to residential property, within 5 days after receiving notification of the date of the hearing by the court the claimant must send a notice to (i) the property, addressed to "the tenant or the occupier"; (ii) the housing department of the local authority within which the property is located;[86] and (iii) any registered proprietor (other than the claimant) of a registered charge over the property.[87] The notice sent to the property must (i) state that a possession claim for the property has started; (ii) show the name and

---

[83] There is no specific provision for such claim on form N120: cf form N119 (Particulars of claim for possession (rented residential property)).

[84] See Chapter 7.

[85] CPR r.55.8(6).

[86] The notice sent to the local authority must state the full address of the property: CPR r.55.10(3A).

[87] CPR r.55.10(2).

address of the claimant, the defendant and the court which issued the claim form; and (iii) give details of the hearing.[88]

3.10 The lender must produce copies of the notices and evidence of service at the hearing.[89] The general rules in CPR Part 6 as to service apply.

3.11 As the claim is for the recovery of land, any other persons who are known to be claiming an independent right to occupy the property should be joined as defendants. This does not mean that all mortgagors need to be joined (if not in occupation of the property) – unless the claim includes a money claim. A spouse who has registered a Class F land charge, notice or caution does not have to be joined as a defendant.[90] However, it is generally advisable to join all known occupiers (whether authorised or not) and mortgagors as defendants.

3.12 Where the mortgagor is deceased, the claim should be issued against the personal representatives of his estate, where a grant of probate or administration has been made, or "the estate of [the mortgagor]" where no such grant has been made.[91] In the latter situation, it will be necessary to make an application under CPR r.19.8(2)(b)(ii) to appoint a person to represent the estate in the claim. Where a mortgagor dies before the proceedings are issued, but proceedings are commenced against him personally, the claim is deemed to have been issued against the mortgagor's

---

[88] CPR r.55.10(3).

[89] CPR r.55.10(4).

[90] However, a 'connected person' (i.e. a spouse, former spouse, civil partner, former civil partner, co-habitant or former co-habitant) may apply to be joined as a defendant under s.55 Family Law Act 1996 'at any time before the action is finally disposed of'. This is discussed further in Chapters 4 and 9.

[91] CPR r.19.8(2).

estate,[92] and it will be necessary to make an application under CPR r.19.8(2)(b)(ii).

3.13 There is no formal requirement for the borrower to file a defence. However, any defence filed should be in the prescribed form. Form N11M (Defence form (mortgaged residential premises[93])) seeks information not only in respect of matters set out in the claim form which are disputed by the defendant, and whether any payments have been made since the claim was issued, but also (i) seeks detailed information as to the mortgagor's financial situation,[94] (ii) asks whether the mortgagor is asking the court to consider whether the terms of the original loan agreement are fair,[95] and (ii) asks whether the mortgagor is intending to apply for a 'time order'.[96]

3.14 A lender cannot obtain default judgment if no defence is filed, nor is a defendant precluded from taking part in any hearing, although failure to file a defence may be taken into account when considering any issue of costs.[97]

Evidence

3.15 Para 5.1 of Practice Direction 55A provides that each party should, where possible, include all evidence he wishes to present in his statement of case, verified by a statement of truth. That does not, however, preclude, evidence being brought up to date

---

[92] CPR r.19.8(3).

[93] An occupier of the property who is not a mortgagor may need to use either Form N11 or N11R (if appropriate) instead.

[94] Including whether the mortgagor is receiving or has applied for income support, dependents, income, savings and regular expenses.

[95] See Chapter 5.

[96] See Chapter 9.

[97] CPR r.55.7.

orally, or in writing, at the hearing,[98] and it is advisable for the lender to file and serve a witness statement shortly before the hearing, which:

(i) Updates the arrears and sums required to redeem the mortgage at the date of the statement and at the date of the hearing if no payments are received in the interim;

(ii) Exhibits a copy of the mortgage deed, and the mortgage agreement/terms and conditions (particularly if relying on breaches other than non-payment of instalments);

(iii) Exhibits any calling-in letter sent to the borrower, or other notices which may have been required under the terms of the mortgage agreement or any tenancy agreement;

(iv) Sets out the steps taken by the lender to comply with the Pre-Action Protocol;

(v) Exhibits an up-to-date search certificate of HM Land Registry[99] or Land Charges Department (the original of the same should be produced at the hearing); and

(vi) Confirms that the requisite notices to occupiers, other chargees and the local housing authority has been sent, and exhibit copies of the same.

3.16 If the mortgage contains an "all monies" clause, and there are monies outstanding in other accounts secured against the property, then the witness statement should also set out the sums outstanding and rate of interest, updated to the date of the hearing, and this figure should be included in the amount necessary to redeem the mortgage.

---

[98] Practice Direction 55A para 5.2.

[99] It is no longer necessary to provide the original charge certificate where the charge is registered on the official copy entry of title: LRA 2002 s.67.

3.17 It should not be necessary for the maker of the statement to attend court – at least at the first hearing – as CPR 55.8(3) provides that except where the claim is allocated to the fast-track or multi-track, or the court orders otherwise, any fact that needs to be proved by the evidence of witnesses may be proved by evidence in writing. However, para 5.4 of Practice Direction 55A provides that if the maker of the statement does not attend the hearing, and the other party disputes material evidence contained in the statement, the court will "normally" adjourn the hearing so that oral evidence can be given. If it is anticipated that that there may be a dispute of fact as to, for example, the terms of the mortgage, the actions taken by the lender, or as to the amounts outstanding/necessary to redeem the mortgage,[100] it would be advisable for the maker of the statement to attend the hearing, although it is unlikely that adjournment will be avoided if the court considers that the claim is genuinely disputed on grounds that seem substantial (in which case it is likely to give case management directions and allocate the claim[101]) or (as is likely to be the case on a first hearing in a possession list) if time does not permit.

3.18 On the other hand, it is likely to be important for the borrower to attend the hearing – particularly where the defence is limited to asking the court to exercise its powers under s.36 of the Administration of Justice Act 1970.[102] The borrower should (inter alia) provide evidence of any outstanding social security or housing benefit payments relevant to the mortgage arrears, the status of any claims for social security or housing benefit about which a decision has not yet been made, and any applications to appeal or review a social security or housing

[100] Although the mortgagee's evidence as to the arrears, account balance and state of the mortgage will usually be accepted: *Landmark Mortgages Ltd v Bamrah* [2017] EWHC 2041 (QB).

[101] CPR r.55.8((1). On the test as to whether the claim is disputed on grounds which appear substantial, see *Global 100 Limited v Laleva* [2021] EWCA Civ 1835.

[102] See Chapter 9.

benefit decision where that appeal or review has not yet concluded.[103]

The hearing

3.19 The hearing date will be not less than 28 days after the claim is issued, but should not be longer than 8 weeks after that date.[104] A date for hearing will be fixed by the court when the claim is issued, unless the claim has been made at a hearing centre not serving the property's address, in which case the hearing date will be fixed when the claim is received by that hearing centre.[105]

3.20 At the hearing, the court may dismiss the claim, grant a possession order, or give directions for the claim. If the claim is genuinely disputed on grounds which appear to be substantial, the claim will be allocated to either the fast track or the multi-track.[106] In making that decision, the court will have regard to a number of matters including the amount of any arrears, the importance of retaining possession to the defendant, the importance of vacant possession to the claimant, and the matters set out in CPR r.26.8 as modified by the relevant practice direction.[107] A claim will not be allocated to the small claims court unless both parties agree.[108] Where the claim is allocated to the fast track or multi track, the court will usually give directions setting the matter down for trial in the usual way.

---

[103] Practice Direction 55A para 5.1.

[104] CPR r.55.5(3).

[105] CPR r.55.5(1) & (1A).

[106] CPR r.55.8(2) read with CPR r.55.9(2).

[107] CPR r.55.9(1).

[108] CPR r.55.9(2).

The Order

3.21 If the court makes an order for possession it will do so in a prescribed form.[109] Where the court makes an 'immediate' order for possession this will usually provide for the defendant to give up possession to the claimant within 28 days. If vacant possession is not provided by the date and time specified in the order, then the mortgagee will need to request a warrant of possession. Such application should be made on form N325[110] in the County Court, certifying that the property has not been vacated in accordance with the order and providing the prescribed information.[111]

3.22 Alternatively, the court may make a suspended possession order, suspending the execution of the order on terms. Where possession is sought following non-compliance with the terms of such order relating to the payment of monies, a request for a warrant of possession should be made on form N325A, certifying the breach, and providing the prescribed information.[112]

3.23 Where applying for a warrant of possession of a dwelling-house subject to a mortgage, the claimant must also certify that notice has been given in accordance with the Dwelling Houses (Execution of Possession of Orders by Mortgagees) Regulations 2010.[113]

---

[109] Form N26, or Form N31 for a suspended possession order (discussed further in Chapter 9).

[110] Request for warrant for possession of land.

[111] See CPR r.83.26.

[112] CPR r.83.26.

[113] CPR r.83.26(5). The Regulations are discussed in Chapter 6.

3.24 For claims in the High Court, the mortgagee will need to apply for a writ of possession.[114]

3.25 The execution, and suspension, of possession orders is discussed in more detail in Chapter 9.

Coronavirus

3.26 On 26 March 2020, Practice Direction 51Z was issued as the 117th Update to the Civil Procedure Rules. The Practice Direction, which came into effect on 27 March 2020, provided that all proceedings for possession brought under CPR Part 55 and all proceedings seeking to enforce an order for possession by a warrant or writ of possession were stayed for a period of 90 days.[115] That period was extended by the replacement of Practice Direction 51Z by a new CPR r.55.29 with effect from 25 June 2020 which provided for a stay on possession claims (with certain exclusions) until 22 August 2020.[116] The stay was then further extended until 20 September 2020.[117]

3.27 Practice Direction 55C, which provides for temporary modification of Part 55, came into effect on 20 September 2020. The majority of its provisions applied to claims brought on or before 19 September 2020 (including an appeal from a decision in such a claim) which was subject to the stay in CPR r.55.29. The Practice Direction continues to have effect, however, after 30 November 2021 (the end of the 'interim period') in relation to claims issued before 1 December 2021

---

[114] CPR r.83.13.

[115] The Practice Direction was amended on 2 April 2020 to exclude certain proceedings from the stay (118th Update to the Civil Procedure Rules). For a discussion of the stay generally, see *Arkin v Marshall* [2020] 1 W.L.R. 3284.

[116] CPR r.55.29 was introduced by the Civil Procedure Rules (Amendment No.2)(Coronavirus) Rules 2020.

[117] CPR r.55.29 being amended by the Civil Procedure Rules (Amendment No.5)(Coronavirus) Rules 2020.

and makes specific provision for 'new claims' issued after 19 September 2020.

3.28 Paras 2.1 – 3.1 provided that for stayed claims issued before 3 August 2020 (other than claims in which a final order for possession had been made) that, unless the court directed otherwise, no such claim was to be listed, relisted, heard, or referred to a judge under CPR r.55.15 unless one of the parties had filed a "reactivation notice" confirming that they wished the case to be listed, relisted, heard or referred.[118] If no reactivation notice had been filed in relation to a stayed claim by 4pm on 30 April 2021, then the claim was automatically stayed.[119] Paras 5.1 – 5.4 make provision for the management of a stayed claim in which case management directions were made before 20 September 2020. Where any trial date was set prior to 27 March 2020, that hearing date is vacated and case stayed unless a party complies with the provisions of paras 2.1, 2.2, 2.4 (updated rent account where claim is based on arrears of rent) and 5.1 not less than 42 days prior to the hearing date.[120] Unless it directs otherwise, the court must give at least 21 days' notice to the parties of any hearing listed or relisted in response to a reactivation notice.[121]

3.29 Para 6.1 applies to any claims (new or stayed) brought on or after 3 August 2020 (and before 21 December 2021) and requires that the claimant bring to a hearing two copies of a notice setting out what knowledge that party has as to the effect of the Coronavirus pandemic on the defendant and their dependents, and serve that notice on the defendant not less than 14 days prior to the hearing.

[118] Paras 2.1 – 2.2.

[119] Para 2.6. Para 2.7 makes clear that that stay is not a sanction for breach, and an application to lift such a stay is not an application for relief from sanctions.

[120] Para 2.5.

[121] Para 3.1.

3.30 Para 6.2, which applies to all claims brought under Part II of CPR Part 55 (Accelerated possession claims of property let on an assured shorthold tenancy) brought on or after 3 August 2020 (and before 21 December 2021) provides that the claimant must file a notice setting out what knowledge that party has as to the effect of the Coronavirus pandemic on the defendant and their dependents with the claim form for service with it.

CHAPTER FOUR

RESIDENTIAL PROPERTY

Requirement for Court Order

4.1 At common law, a mortgagee does not require a court order in order to take possession or to sell the mortgaged property.[122] However, it is unlawful to enforce a mortgage that is a regulated mortgage contract, a regulated agreement or a exempt consumer credit agreement that would otherwise be a regulated agreement without a court order.[123] It is also an offence under s.6 of the Criminal Law Act 1977 for a person, without lawful authority, to use or threaten violence for the purpose of securing entrance, for himself or any other person, into any premises if there is someone present at the premises who opposes entry and he knows that to be the case. In practice, this means that whenever possession is sought of a mortgaged residential property, it is likely that a possession order will be required.

The Pre-Action Protocol

4.2 The Mortgage Arrears Pre-Action Protocol for Possession Claims Based on Mortgage or Home Purchase Plan Arrears in Respect of Residential Property (the Pre-Action Protocol) came into force on 19th November 2008. [124] It was introduced against a backdrop of possession claims of residential property based on mortgage arrears having increased year on year to the point where they exceeded residential landlord and tenant

[122] *Ropaigealach v Barclays Bank Plc* [2000] Q.B. 263.

[123] CCA 1974 s.126(1).

[124] Available on the Ministry of Justice website (https://www.justice.gov.uk/courts/procedure-rules/civil/protocol/prot_mha) at date of writing

claims in the third quarter of 2007,[125] and a growing concern from the press, and from Parliament, that 'something must be done'.

4.3 The Pre-Action Protocol is intended to encourage mortgage lenders and borrowers to engage with each other as soon as the borrower starts falling into arrears with a view to avoiding possession proceedings, whilst recognising that, in some cases, an order for possession might be in the best interests of both the lender and the borrower.[126]

4.4 The Pre-Action Protocol applies to:

(i) First charge residential mortgages and home purchase plans[127] regulated by the Financial Services Authority under the Financial Services and Markets Act 2000 (as amended by the Financial Services Act 2012);

(ii) Second charge mortgages over residential property and other secured loans regulated under the Consumer Credit Act 1974 on residential property; and

(iii) Unregulated residential mortgages.

4.5 The Pre-Action Protocol does not apply to Buy-to-Let mortgages.[128]

4.6 The Pre-Action Protocol does not affect the parties' strict legal rights,[129] but it may have some effect on how quickly a

---

[125] Page 11 of the Civil Justice Council Consultation Paper on the Mortgage Arrears Protocol (2008).

[126] Para 2.3 of the Pre-Action Protocol.

[127] Defined in para 1.1(b) as "a method of purchasing a property by way of a sale and lease arrangement that does not require the payment of interest".

[128] Para 4.3 of the Pre-Action Protocol.

[129] Para 1.2 of the Pre-Action Protocol.

mortgagee can obtain possession – particularly if the steps set out in it are not followed. The Pre-Action Protocol stresses that starting possession proceedings should be a *"last resort"* and a claim *"must not normally be started unless all other reasonable attempts to resolve the situation have failed"*[130] and the parties are encouraged to consider whether, depending on the borrower's circumstances, it would be appropriate to:

(i) Extend the term of the mortgage;

(ii) Change the type of the mortgage;

(iii) Capitalise the arrears; or

(iv) Make use of any Government forbearance initiatives in which the lender chooses to participate.

4.7 Paras 5.1 to 5.8 of the Pre-Action Protocol set out the steps which should be taken by both parties as soon as the borrower starts falling into arrears.

4.8 Firstly, the lender is required to provide the borrower with certain information on the arrears,[131] including:

(i) The total amount of the arrears;

(ii) The total outstanding on the mortgage or the home purchase plan; and

(iii) Whether interest or charges will be added, and if so and where appropriate, details or an estimate of the interest or charges that may be payable.

4.9 In addition, the lender must:

---

130 Para 7.1 of the Pre-Action Protocol.

131 Para 5.1 (c) of the Pre-Action Protocol.

(i) Where appropriate, provide the borrower with the required regulatory information sheet or the National Homelessness Advice Service / Shelter / Cymru booklet on mortgage arrears;[132]

(ii) Provide information on the current monthly instalments and the amounts paid for the last two years;[133]

(iii) Advise the borrower to make early contact with the housing department of the borrower's local authority and should, where relevant, refer the borrower to appropriate sources of independent debt advice.[134]

4.10 The lender should also seek information about whether the property is occupied by an "authorised tenant"[135]: i.e. a tenant whose tenancy is authorised as between the borrower and the lender.[136] In practice, this is likely to be a tenant who was in situ at the date the mortgage was granted; whose identity and/or tenancy was notified to, and/or approved by, the lender prior to the grant of the tenancy agreement where that is a condition of the mortgage agreement; or a tenant whose tenancy was otherwise granted in accordance with the terms of the mortgage agreement.

4.11 The Pre-Action Protocol requires that when either party attempts to communicate and provide information, *"reasonable steps should be taken to do so in a way that is clear, fair and not misleading."* In particular, *"If the lender is aware that the borrower may have difficulties in reading or understanding the information*

[132] Para 5.1(a) of the Pre-Action Protocol.

[133] Para 5.1 (b) of the Pre-Action Protocol.

[134] Para 5.3 of the Pre-Action Protocol.

[135] Para 5.2 of the Pre-Action Protocol.

[136] Para 1.1(e) of the Pre-Action Protocol.

provided, the lender should take reasonable steps to ensure that information is provided in a way that the borrower can understand."[137]

4.12 The Pre-Action Protocol also provides that the parties, or their representatives, should take *"all reasonable steps to discuss with each other the reasons for the arrears, the borrower's financial circumstances and proposals for repayment of the arrears"*.[138] The parties should, for example, consider whether the reason for the arrears are temporary, or long-term, and whether the borrower may be able to repay them within a reasonable time.

4.13 If the borrower makes a "*reasonable request*" to change the date of regular payment (within the same payment period) or the method by which payments are to be made, the lender must consider the same. Where the lender does not accept the request, he must provide the borrower with written reasons for refusal,within a reasonable period of so doing.[139]

4.14 Similarly, if the borrower makes a proposal for payment, the lender must respond to the same "*promptly*" and, where he does not agree to the proposal, must give the borrower reasons in writing within 10 business days.[140]

4.15 If the proposal emanates from the lender, then the lender must "*set out the proposal in sufficient detail to enable the borrower to understand the implications of the proposal*" and give the borrower "*a reasonable period of time*" in which to consider the same.[141]

4.16 If the borrower fails to comply with an agreement, the lender

[137] Para 2.2 of the Pre-Action Protocol.

[138] Para 5.4 of the Pre-Action Protocol.

[139] Para 5.5 of the Pre-Action Protocol.

[140] Para 5.6 of the Pre-Action Protocol.

[141] Para 5.7 of the Pre-Action Protocol.

should warn the borrower of his intention to commence possession proceedings by giving the borrower 15 business days' notice in writing, unless the agreement provides otherwise.[142]

4.17 The Pre-Action Protocol advises that a lender *"must not"* consider starting a claim for possession where the borrower can demonstrate to the lender that he has:

(a) submitted a claim to–

(i) the Department for Works and Pensions ('DWP') for Support for Mortgage Interest (SMI) or, if appropriate, Universal Credit; or

(ii) an insurer under a mortgage payment protection policy; or

(iii) a participating local authority for support under a Mortgage Rescue Scheme, or other means of homelessness prevention support provided by the local authority,

and has provided all the evidence required to process a claim;

(b) a reasonable expectation of eligibility for payment from the DWP or from an insurer or support from the local authority or welfare or charitable organisation such as the Veterans Welfare Scheme or Royal British Legion;

(c) an ability to pay a mortgage instalment not covered by a claim to the DWP or the insurer in relation to such a claim;

(d) difficulty in respect of affordability or another specific personal or financial difficulty, and requires time to seek

[142] Para 5.8 of the Pre-Action Protocol.

free independent debt advice, or has a confirmed appointment with a debt adviser and

(e) a reasonable expectation, providing evidence where possible, of an improvement in their financial circumstances in the foreseeable future (for example a new job or increased income from a lodger). [143]

4.18 A lender must also consider postponing a claim to allow the borrower a realistic period of time to sell the property if the borrower can demonstrate that reasonable steps have been taken, or will be taken, to market the property at an appropriate price in accordance with reasonable professional advice.[144] If the lender agrees to postpone starting the claim, the borrower must continue to take all reasonable steps to actively market the property, and should provide the lender with copies of the particulars of sale,[145] details of purchase offers received within a reasonable period of time specified by the lender, and details of the estate agent and conveyancer instructed to deal with the sale.[146]

4.19 Where the lender decides not to postpone the start of a possession claim he should inform the borrower of the reasons for this decision at least 5 business days before starting proceedings.[147]

4.20 The lender must also consider whether to postpone commencing possession proceedings where the borrower has made a genuine complaint to the Financial Ombudsman

---

[143] Paras 6.1 and 6.2 of the Pre-Action Protocol.

[144] Para 6.2 of the Pre-Action Protocol.

[145] And the Energy Performance Certificate or proof that one has been commissioned.

[146] Para 6.3 of the Pre-Action Protocol.

[147] The borrower should also authorise the estate agent and conveyancer to communicate with the lender about the progress of the sale and the borrower's conduct during the process.

Service about the potential possession claim.[148] Where the lender does not intend to await the outcome of the Ombudsman proceedings, the lender must give the borrower notice, with reasons, that he intends to commence possession proceedings.[149]

4.21 Whilst there are no express sanctions for non-compliance set out in the Pre-Action Protocol itself, the court will expect to be informed what actions have been taken to comply with the same at any hearing for possession. It is advisable for the lender to set out, either in a witness statement or in the particulars of claim, what steps have been taken to communicate with the borrower and, if any proposal has been refused, to explain why. The lender is required to bring two copies of the completed checklist (N123) to the hearing.

4.22 As discussed above, the Pre-Action Protocol, does not affect the parties' legal rights and obligations – and non-compliance with the Protocol will not, in and of itself, provide a substantive defence to the proceedings. However, it is likely that that a failure by a lender to take any of the steps set out in the Protocol will result in a delay in its ability to obtain the order it seeks, with the court potentially staying or adjourning proceedings to enable the requirements to be complied with (for example, for the lender to consider a proposal by the borrower, or for the borrower to attempt to sell the property). It may also be relevant to the exercise of the court's jurisdiction under the Administration of Justice Act 1970 or Consumer Credit Act 1974 (see Chapter 9). It might also provide a basis for disallowing the lender's costs. If the lender has not complied with the Protocol, and the Court adjourns the hearing on that basis, the borrower may want to consider asking the court to direct that the lender is not entitled to add to its security the

[148] Para 8.1 of the Pre-Action Protocol.

[149] Para 8.2 of the Pre-Action Protocol.

costs of that hearing.[150]

4.23 Having regard to the above, it is clear that the importance of the lender taking pro-active steps to interact with the borrower, and seeking to reach some sort of agreement as to how repossession could be avoided, cannot be over-emphasised when the lender is considering starting a claim for possession.

Family Property

4.24 As outlined in Chapter 3, when commencing a claim for possession of residential property, the claimant is required to state in the particulars of claim whether:

(i) A Class F land charge has been registered under section 2(7) of the Matrimonial Homes Act 1967;

(ii) A notice registered under section 2(8) or 8(3) of the Matrimonial Homes Act 1983 has been entered and on whose behalf; or

(iii) A notice under section 31(10) of the Family Law Act 1996 has been registered and on whose behalf.

4.25 Essentially these charges and notice all relate to interests of non-property owning spouses or civil partners against property owned by their spouse or civil partner, or former spouse or civil partner.

4.26 Section 30 of the Family Law Act 1996 (FLA 1996) applies where one spouse or civil partner ('A') is entitled to occupy a dwelling-house by virtue of (i) a beneficial estate or interest or contract; or (ii) any enactment giving A the right to remain in occupation, and the other spouse or civil partner ('B') is not so entitled.[151] Subject to the following provisions of s.30, s.30(2)

[150] On costs generally, see Chapter 7.

[151] FLA 1996 s.30(9) provides that a person (a) who has an equitable interest in the dwelling-house or in its proceeds of sale but (b) is not a person in whom there is

confers two identified rights on B, now known as "home rights" (originally "matrimonial home rights"):

(i) If in occupation, a right not to be evicted or excluded from the dwelling-house or any part of it except with the leave of the court given by an order under section 33;

(ii) If not in occupation, a right with the leave of the court so given to enter into and occupy the dwelling-house.

4.27 Those rights do not apply where the dwellinghouse was at no time used, or intended to be used, by A and B as their matrimonial or civil partnership home.[152] Home rights subsist (i) only so long as the marriage, or civil partnership, subsists except to the extent that an order under FLA 1996 s.33(5) provides otherwise, and (ii) only so long as A is entitled (as provided for under s.30(1)) to occupy the dwellinghouse, except where provision is made by FLA 1996 s.31 for those rights to be a charge on the estate or interest.[153] Even when protected by a charge under s.31, the rights are brought to an end on the death of A, or termination of the marriage or civil partnership, unless the court directs otherwise by an order to that effect made under s.33(5).[154]

4.28 Section 31(1) and (2) provide that where home rights exist, they are a charge on A's estate or interest in the matrimonial or civil partnership home. If the property is registered at HM Land Registry, and the charge is against a legal estate, then the charge

---

vested (whether solely or as joint tenant) a legal estate in fee simple or a legal term of years absolute in the dwelling-house, is to be treated, only for the purposes of determining whether he has home rights, as not being entitled to occupy the dwelling-house by virtue of that interest.

[152] FLA 1996 s.30(7).

[153] FLA 1996 s.30(8).

[154] FLA 1996 s.31(8).

is protected by entry of a notice on the title.[155] If the property is unregistered, then the charge should be registered as a Class F land charge, provided the charge is against a legal estate.[156]

4.29 The charge has the same effect as if it was an equitable interested created at the later of (a) the date on which A acquired the estate or interest, (b) the date of marriage or formation of the civil partnership, or (c) 1 January 1968.[157] Where the property is subject to a mortgage, if the Class F charge is subsequently registered, then the home rights charge will be deemed to be a mortgage subsequent in date to that first charge for the purposes of LPA 1925 s.94. Home rights are not overriding interests for the purposes of LRA 2002 Schedule 3.[158]

4.30 A Class F land charge registered under s.2(7) of the Matrimonial Homes Act 1967 or notice registered under s.2(8) of the Matrimonial Homes Act 1983 are essentially to the same effect, securing the occupation rights of a non-property owning spouse over a matrimonial home. Notices and cautions registered under s.2 of either Act were unaffected by the coming into force of the LRA 2002.[159]

4.31 Home rights do not confer on spouse or civil partner B any greater right to occupy the property against a mortgagee than are enjoyed by spouse or civil partner A,[160] unless their rights are a charge affecting the mortgagee on the estate or interest charged.[161] Similarly, former spouses or civil partners, who may

---

155 FLA 1996 s.31(10).

156 FLA 1996 s.31(13), read with s.2 of the Land Charges Act 1972.

157 FLA 1996 s.31(3).

158 FLA 1996 s.31(10).

159 LRA 2002 s.134(2) and Sch 12 para 1.

160 FLA 1996 s.54(3).

161 FLA 1996 s.54(4).

enjoy similar rights to occupy the property pursuant to an order made under FLA 1996 ss.35 or 36 do not enjoy any greater right to occupy the property against a mortgagee than are enjoyed by their former spouse or civil partner.[162]

4.32 However, where a claim for possession is commenced by a mortgagee, a "connected person" (i.e. a spouse, former spouse, civil partner, former civil partner, co-habitant or former co-habitant[163] of the mortgagor) may apply to be joined as a defendant under FLA 1996 s.55[164] and is entitled to be made a party in the circumstances set out in s.55(3), i.e.:

(a) The connected person is enabled by FLA 1996 s.30(3) or (6) (or by s.30(3) or (6) as applied by ss.35(13) or 36(13)), to meet the mortgagor's liabilities under the mortgage;

(b) he has applied to the court before the action is finally disposed of in that court; and

(c) the court sees no special reason against his being made a party to the action and is satisfied—

(i) that he may be expected to make such payments or do such other things in or towards satisfaction of the mortgagor's liabilities or obligations as might affect the outcome of the proceedings; or

(ii) that the expectation of it should be considered under section 36 of the Administration of Justice Act 1970.

[162] FLA 1996 s.54(3).

[163] FLA 1996 s.54(5).

[164] FLA 1996 s.55(2).

4.33 The reference to a person being "enabled" to meet the mortgagor's liabilities under the mortgage is a reference to the proviso in FLA 1996 s.30(3) (applied to trust properties by s.30(6)) that any payment (etc) by B in satisfaction of a liability for a mortgage payment affecting a dwelling house is as good as if it were done by A. Similar provisions are made in respect of a former spouse or civil partner in s.35(13) and for a cohabitant or former cohabitant in s.36(13).

4.34 A person enjoying home rights (or similar rights pursuant to a court order under ss.35 or 36) may therefore be able to prevent an order for possession being made, if they can satisfy the court that they can pay any sums due under the mortgage, and the court is satisfied that it should exercise its jurisdiction under the AJA 1970 to either adjourn the proceedings, or to stay or suspend execution of any possession order on terms.

Administration of Justice Acts 1970 and 1973

4.35 AJA 1970 s.36, read with AJA 1973 s.8 confers a power on a court seized with a claim for possession of residential property to adjourn proceedings, or, on making an order for possession, to stay or suspend execution of the order or postpone the date for delivery of possession for such period or periods as it thinks reasonable, where it is satisfied that if those powers are exercised the mortgagor is likely to be able, within a reasonable period, to pay any sums due under the mortgage or to remedy a default consisting of a breach of any other obligation under the mortgage. These powers do not apply where the mortgage is a regulated agreement under CCA 1974 but do apply to regulated mortgage contracts under FSMA 2000. These powers are discussed in more detail in Chapter 9.

CHAPTER FIVE

DEFENCES

5.1 As outlined in Chapter 1, there are a number of matters which may qualify or restrict a mortgagee's entitlement to possession. This Chapter considers a number of the defences which might be available in an appropriate case to defeat a claim for possession. The court's discretion to suspend a possession order, or execution of an order, is considered separately: see Chapter 9.

General points to consider

5.2 There are three points which any mortgagor faced with a claim for possession would be advised to consider at the outset.

5.3 Firstly, is the mortgage enforceable?

5.4 As discussed in Chapter 2, if the mortgage agreement is a regulated mortgage contract, a home purchase plan, or a regulated agreement, and has not been granted by a person authorised to grant such agreements by the FCA, then the agreement will be unenforceable by the mortgagee against the mortgagor unless the court orders otherwise. The Court will only make such an order if it is satisfied that it is just and equitable in the circumstances of the case to do so.[165] Where the agreement is made by an unauthorised person,[166] in making that decision the court is required to consider whether the person carrying on the regulated activity reasonably believed

[165] FSMA 2000 s.28(3).

[166] As opposed to 'through' an unauthorised person, on which, see FSMA 2000 s.27.

that he was not contravening the general prohibition by making the agreement.[167]

5.5 In *Helden v Strathmore Ltd* [2011] H.L.R. 41, the trial judge identified the following factors as relevant to that question, and as justifying an order that the agreement was enforceable in that case:

(i) The claimant had had the use of the property which the defendant's loan enabled him to buy since 2006 without making rent or interest payments;

(ii) The property had increased substantially in value. The loan from the defendant had therefore enabled the claimant to make a large profit;

(iii) The defendant would not have been willing to make the loan on an unsecured basis;

(iv) The defendant could have expected to have generated a return on the money lent to the claimant by investing it elsewhere, and had lost that potential profit as a result of lending the money to the claimant;

(v) There was no question of the claimant having been taken advantage of. The claimant had considerable experience in property matters including as a mortgage broker. The claimant and defendant had agreed the rates of interest to be charged, which were not exorbitant;

(vi) The claimant had preferred not to pursue alternative funding because of his concern that he should be able to make lump sum payments without penalty;

[167] FSMA 2000 s.28(4) & (5).

(vii) The claimant had not identified any respects in which he would have been better placed if the defendant had been authorised under the FSMA.[168]

5.6 That analysis was summarised in *Jackson v Ayles*[169] [2021] EWHC 995 (Ch) as the court *"weighing the respective sophistication and experience of the parties, whether the borrower was taken advantage of, motivation for the borrowing and if he benefited from the transaction"*.[170] The judge (Chief ICC Judge Briggs) also stressed the language 'just and equitable' in the context of unregulated lending and the FSMA.[171] The judge found that the mortgagee whose charge was secured over the property could not have reasonably believed that he was not contravening the general prohibition in making the agreement,[172] and this was a *"weighty factor against the grant of relief"*.[173] If he had been able to make good a contention that he so believed or that his belief was reasonable, and thus could have availed himself of the provision in FSMA s.28(5), *"it would not necessarily have meant that relief should be granted but as he has not satisfied the provision he must demonstrate circumstances that*

[168] [2010] EWHC 2012 (Ch) at para 100, discussed by the Court of Appeal at para 45. The Court of Appeal left open the question of whether the fact that the defendant was unaware of the fact that the FSMA applied to them (and, as the trial judge (Newey J) had found, that it was reasonable for them to do so) was a relevant factor.

[169] Ms Jackson was the Trustee-in-Bankruptcy for the first named defendant, Stephen Ayles. The case was an application in the bankruptcy proceedings seeking a declaration that security held over the matrimonial home of Mr and Mrs Ayles (the first and second named defendants) by Mr Pumphrey (the third named defendant) was unenforceable pursuant to the FSMA 2000. A challenge was also made to a second charge over the property, in the name of Mr and Mrs Pumphrey (the fourth named defendant) on different grounds.

[170] Para 22.

[171] Para 22.

[172] The "issue" in FSMA 2000 s.28(5) to which the court is to have regard under s.28(4)(a).

[173] Para 55.

outweigh the "weighty factor" and it is "just and equitable" to enforce". The judge did not consider the circumstances relied on by the defendant were sufficient to outweigh the *"weighty factor"* against the grant of relief in that case.[174]

5.7 Secondly, have the conditions which give rise to an entitlement to seek possession arisen?

5.8 This will require careful reading of the mortgage agreement. By way of example:

(i) If the mortgage is payable in instalments, is there a requirement for a certain level of arrears to have arisen before possession proceedings can be commenced?

(ii) Is there a requirement for the principal sum to be demanded, or a letter sent to the mortgagor calling in the monies due, before possession proceedings can be commenced? If so, have those formalities been complied with?

(iii) If possession is to be sought on grounds of breach of another condition of the mortgage, does the mortgage agreement require that the mortgagor first be given an opportunity to remedy the breach? If so, has that requirement been complied with?

(iv) If the mortgage agreement requires the mortgagor to be given notice of intended proceedings, has that notice been given and relevant timescales elapsed prior to the claim being issued?

5.9 Thirdly, as legal mortgages granted post October 2003 are required to be completed by registration,[175] the mortgagor in receipt of a claim (and mortgagee planning to commence one)

---

[174] Para 55. Those factors were discussed at paras 37-45 of the judgment.

[175] See para 1.3 above.

would be advised to check that the mortgagee is properly registered as proprietor of the charge at HM Land Registry. Problems with the registration of a charge (or its non-registration) can more be easily be dealt with at HM Land Registry rather than during the course of possession proceedings.

Good faith

5.10 Whilst the mortgagee may have the right to seek possession of the property, that does not mean he can do so for any purpose. The power must be exercised in good faith, for the purpose of enforcing or preserving the security for the mortgagee's liability. The power may not be used for a collateral purpose.[176] The court may, for example, decline to grant a possession order against one mortgagor if a joint mortgagor, also in occupation, appears to have a substantive defence against the mortgagee,[177] or where granting possession against a mortgagor would otherwise be ineffective to enforce his security or to confer any tangible benefit on the mortgagor.

Imperfect or irregular documentation

5.11 Where an apparent signatory to a mortgage deed or agreement claims that the signature was not his (having been forged, or signed by a third party without his agreement) or that whilst he physically signed the document he did so believing it to be of a fundamentally different nature, that may provide a defence of non est factum.

5.12 Where it is claimed that the signature is not that of the alleged signatory, it will usually be necessary to adduce expert evidence to the support the defence, most likely that of a handwriting expert (showing that someone other than the defendant signed

[176] See, for example, *Quennell v Maltby* [1979] 1 W.L.R. 318; *Midland Bank Plc v McGrath* [1996] EGCS 61

[177] *Albany Home Loans Ltd v Massey* [1997] 2 All E.R. 609

the document) or other forensic expert (for example, if it is suggested that the signature was not originally attached to the document in dispute).

5.13 Where it is claimed that the defendant signed the document believing it to be something else, the defendant will need to show *"a radical or fundamental difference between what [he] signed and what he thought he was signing".*[178] The court has previously held that an "all monies charge" is sufficiently different from a guarantee relating to monies borrowed to fund a specific purchase for the defence to apply.[179] The onus is on the defendant, however, to demonstrate that he took all reasonable care to ascertain the nature and meaning of the document before signing it.[180] This is likely to mean, in practice, that it will be difficult for an adult of full capacity to establish such a defence – absent some sort of trickery.

5.14 The effect of a successful defence of non est factum is that the mortgage is void – regardless of fault on the part of the other contacting party. Where the charge is registered at HM Land Registry, it will still be necessary to apply for rectification of the register. The court retains a discretion whether to make such an order, and may decline to do so in exceptional circumstances.[181]

Misrepresentation

5.15 Where a mortgagor has been induced to enter into the mortgage by misrepresentation, that may also provide grounds for the mortgage to be set aside. That is the case even in the event of an innocent (as opposed to fraudulent) misrepresentation.[182]

---

178 *Saunders v Anglia Building Society* [1971] 1 A.C. 1004 at pg 1017.

179 *Lloyds Bank Plc v Waterhouse* [1993] 2 F.L.R. 97.

180 That of a *"normal man of prudence": Saunders v Anglia Building Society* at 1027.

181 See, for example, *Dhillon v Barclays Bank Plc* [2020] EWCA Civ 619.

182 *TSB Bank Plc v Camfield* [1995] 1 W.L.R. 430.

Whilst the misrepresentation does not have to have been made by the mortgagee, the mortgage is only liable to be set aside if the mortgagee had actual or constructive knowledge of the misrepresentation.[183] Essentially, the circumstances in which a mortgagee will be put on inquiry (and thereafter at risk of having a mortgage set aside, if misrepresentation is established) are[184]:

(i) Under the mortgage, the defendant has stood as surety for the debts of a spouse or partner,[185] or other cohabitee;

(ii) The transaction is not, on the face of it, to the defendant's benefit;

(iii) The mortgagee has not taken reasonable steps to satisfy himself that the surety entered into the agreement freely and in knowledge of the true facts. This is discussed further below.

Undue influence

5.16 A mortgage may also be set aside if a mortgagor can establish that it was entered into as a result of undue influence, the mortgagee was on notice of the undue influence, and did not take reasonable steps to ascertain that the mortgage was being entered into freely and in knowledge of the true facts.

5.17 As with misrepresentation, the undue influence does not need to be exercised by the mortgagee on the mortgagor, but may be exercised by one mortgagor over another, or even by someone

---

[183] *O'Brien v Barclays Bank Plc* [1994] 1 A.C. 180

[184] *O'Brien* at pg 198.

[185] Including a company owned by the spouse or partner. The House of Lords made clear in *O'Brien* that relationship between others, such as a son and elderly parents, might be of the same kind as that between a husband and wife, for the purposes of this doctrine.

who is not party to the mortgage but who had an interest in the transaction going ahead. The essence of an allegation of undue influence is that the wronged party was not truly consenting to the transaction because another had used a position of influence or domination over them to cause them to enter into the mortgage.

5.18 The defence of undue influence is usually divided into two categories: actual undue influence and presumed undue influence.

5.19 In terms of actual undue influence, this will be for the defendant to establish on the facts of the case. In order to establish a defence of actual undue influence, the defendant will need to establish that:

(i) The wrongdoer had the capacity to influence the defendant;

(ii) The wrongdoer exercised that influence;

(iii) The exercise of that influence was 'undue' – in the sense of wrongdoer taking unfair advantage of the defendant, or depriving the other of free use of independent and informed judgment; and

(iv) The exercise of that influence brought about the transaction.[186]

5.20 As to presumed undue influence, this arises where there is a relationship between the parties by which one party is presumed to have a measure of influence over the other, and the transaction is one which calls for an explanation. As Lord Nicholls explained in *Royal Bank of Scotland Plc v Etridge (No 2)* [2002] 2 A.C. 773:

[186] *Bank of Credit and Commercial International SA v Aboody* [1990] 1 Q.B. 923 per Slade L.J. at pg 967 and see, on point (iii), the more detailed discussed at pgs 967-8.

"The law has adopted a sternly protective attitude towards certain types of relationship in which one party acquires influence over another who is vulnerable and dependent and where, moreover, substantial gifts by the influenced or vulnerable person are not normally to be expected. Examples of relationships within this special class are parent and child, guardian and ward, trustee and beneficiary, solicitor and client, and medical adviser and patient. In these cases the law presumes, irrebuttably, that one party had influence over the other. The complainant need not prove he actually reposed trust and confidence in the other party. It is sufficient for him to prove the existence of the type of relationship."[187]

5.21 There are two broad situations in which a presumption of undue influence may arise. The first, is where the parties are in a certain type of relationship (discussed in *Etridge (No 2)* above) where undue influence will be presumed (the party only has to establish the existence of that relationship). The second, is where there was a relationship between the parties in which the one reposed particular trust and confidence in the other, it being for the party claiming undue influence to establish that such a relationship of trust and confidence existed.

5.22 Where a presumption of undue influence is established, then the burden shifts to the other party to the transaction to show that it was entered into with the "*full, free and informed consent*" of the person alleging undue influence. The most common way of seeking to rebut the presumption is to establish that that person had the benefit of independent legal advice, although other professional advice *may* suffice, depending on the circumstances of the case. A mortgage may be set aside against an innocent third party (such as a bank) where that party had actual, imputed,[188] or constructive knowledge of the undue influence. The seminal guidance on what is required, and the

[187] Per Lord Nicholls at pg 797. The relationship between husband and wife is not such a relationship.

[188] I.e. where knowledge of an agent is imputed to a principal.

steps which a third party can take to protect its position, remains that provided by Lord Nicolls in *Etridge (No 2)*.[189]

5.23 Whilst a claim of undue defence may render the mortgage liable to be set aside, it will not defeat a claim for possession in every case. The mortgage will, for example, remain enforceable where the funds were used to pay off an earlier mortgage which bound the mortgagor, the mortgagee being entitled to enforce the mortgage by way of subrogation,[190] or where the charge is acknowledged in ancillary relief proceedings in connection with a divorce.[191]

Estoppel

5.24 A defence of promissory estoppel may be available in an appropriate case. In *Royal Bank of Scotland Plc v Luwum* [2008] EWCA Civ 648, for example, the bank had agreed that the mortgagor could have 3 months to bring his loan account within the facility limit, and if he did so, the bank would allow him to continue to enjoy the facility as if there had been no default. In reliance on the same, the mortgagor raised funds from third parties, but the bank proceeded to commence possession proceedings. The Court of Appeal overturned the possession order granted by the trial judge on the basis that the bank had become estopped from commencing the claim. Each case will, however, very much depend on its own facts.

5.25 A mortgagor may also be able to rely on a cause of action estoppel (or res judicata) if a mortgagee seeks possession of a property based on arrears in respect of which it had previously, and separately, obtained a monetary judgment.[192] Considerable care should be taken, therefore, if a mortgagee enjoys an "all

[189] See pgs 804-810.

[190] *Castle Phillips Finance Co Ltd v Piddington* [1995] 1 F.L.R. 783.

[191] *First National Bank v Walker* [2001] 1 W.L.R. 505.

[192] *Commercial First Business Ltd v Munday* [2015] 1 P. & C.R. 7.

monies" clause secured over more than one property in terms of any claim that may be pursued, and its terms.

5.26 A defence of estoppel by convention, or waiver, may also be available in principle, but perhaps unlikely to arise in practice. Such an estoppel may arise where both parties to a transaction act on an assumed state of facts or law, or an assumption made by one and acquiesced in by the other,[193] or where a party knows of or acquiesces in a state of affairs (for example, non-compliance with the terms of the mortgage) for a prolonged period of time.

Limitation

5.27 A mortgagee may not bring a claim for possession of a property more than 12 years after the right to enforce the security arose.[194] If the right to take possession was not restricted by the mortgage agreement (for example, to be exercised only in the event of a default or in the event that the moneys loaned were not repaid at the end of the term) this will be 12 years from the date the mortgage was granted.[195] Time will begin to run anew whenever a payment, or part payment is made towards the mortgage debt.[196]

Redemption of mortgage

5.28 A claim for possession will be defeated if, prior to the hearing, the mortgage is repaid in full by the mortgagor; by a spouse, civil partner, former spouse or civil partner, cohabitee or former cohabitee;[197] or by any other person with an interest in the

---

[193] See, for example, *Republic of India v India Steamship Co* [1998] A.C. 878.

[194] Limitation Act 1980 s.15

[195] *Ashe v National Westminster Bank Plc* [2008] 1 W.L.R. 710.

[196] Ibid at para 44; and Limitation Act 1980 s.29.

[197] See paras 4.32 – 4.34 above.

property, who has the right to take a transfer of the mortgage on paying off the loan.[198]

Interests of third parties

5.29 There are some circumstances in which the interest of third parties may defeat a claim for possession of the property. These are discussed in Chapter 6 below.

Consumer protection and unfair contract terms

5.30 As set out in Chapter 2 above, where a mortgage is a regulated mortgage contract under FSMA 2000 or a regulated agreement under CCA 1974, the powers under Part 9 CCA 1974 will be available to the court. In the context of possession claims, the most relevant power is that under s.129 to make a 'time order'. This is discussed below in Chapter 9. The court also has powers to control 'unfair relationships' between a creditor and debtor, i.e. an agreement which is unfair to the debtor because of (a) any of the terms of the agreement or any related agreement; (b) the way in which the creditor has exercised or enforced any of his rights under the agreement or any related agreement; or (c) any other thing done, or not done, by or on behalf of the creditor under the agreement or any related agreement.[199] These powers, which are set out in CCA 1974 s.140B, do not apply to regulated mortgage contracts or home purchase plans.[200] They may, however, be available in respect of a credit agreement[201] secured by a mortgage over land, which is not a

[198] *Tarn v Turner* (1888) 39 Ch.D 456 discussed in *Britannia Building Society v Earl* [1990] 1 W.L.R. 422.

[199] See CCA 1974 s.140A(1). The term "related agreement" is defined in CCA 1974 s.140C(4).

[200] CCA 1974 s.140A(5).

[201] CCA 1974 s.140C(1) defines "credit agreement" for the purposes of s.140A and s.140B as meaning "*any agreement between an individual (the 'debtor') and any other person (the 'creditor') by which the creditor provides the debtor with credit of any amount*".

regulated mortgage contract (or home purchase plan) under FSMA 2000.

5.31 The powers under s.140B may be exercised on an application by the debtor or a surety (which must be made in the County Court[202]); at the instance of the debtor or a surety in any proceedings to which the debtor and creditor are parties, being proceedings to enforcement the agreement (this would include a claim for possession of the property); or at the instance of a creditor or debtor in any other proceedings in any court where the amount paid or payable under the agreement or any related agreement is relevant.[203] The powers may be exercised even after the relationship at issue has ended.[204]

5.32 An order under s.140B may:

(i) require the creditor, or any associate or former associate of his, to repay (in whole or in part) any sum paid by the debtor or by a surety by virtue of the agreement or any related agreement (whether paid to the creditor, the associate or the former associate or to any other person);

(ii) require the creditor, or any associate or former associate of his, to do or not to do (or to cease doing) anything specified in the order in connection with the agreement or any related agreement;

(iii) reduce or discharge any sum payable by the debtor or by a surety by virtue of the agreement or any related agreement;

It is not, therefore, expressly limited to credit agreements which would be regulated agreements under the Act.

202 CA 1974 s.140B(4).

203 CCA 1974 s.140B(2).

204 CCA s.140A(4).

(iv) direct the return to a surety of any property provided by him for the purposes of a security;

(v) otherwise set aside (in whole or in part) any duty imposed on the debtor or on a surety by virtue of the agreement or any related agreement;

(vi) alter the terms of the agreement or of any related agreement;

(vii) direct accounts to be taken between any persons.

5.33 In deciding whether to make an order, the court will have regard to all the matters it considers relevant.[205] Helpful guidance was provided by the Supreme Court in _Plevin v Paragon Personal Finance Ltd_ [2014] 1 W.L.R. 4222. Although the Court was at pains to stress that CCA 1974 s.140A was deliberately framed in wide terms, and it was not possible to state a *"precise or universal test"* for its application, it identified 4 general points for consideration:

(i) *"First, what must be unfair is the relationship between the debtor and the creditor. In a case like the present one, where the terms themselves are not intrinsically unfair, this will often be because the relationship is so one-sided as substantially to limit the debtor's ability to choose."*

(ii) *"Secondly, although the court is concerned with hardship to the debtor, subsection 140A(2) envisages that matters relating to the creditor or the debtor may also be relevant. There may be features of the transaction which operate harshly against the debtor but it does not necessarily follow that the relationship is unfair. These features may be required in order to protect what the court regards as a legitimate interest of the creditor."*

[205] CCA 1974 s.140A(2).

(iii) "*Thirdly, the alleged unfairness must arise from one of the three categories of cause listed at sub-paragraphs (a) to (c).*" (i.e. CCA 1974 s.140(A)(1)(a) – (c) set out at para 5.32 above);

(iv) "*Fourthly, the great majority of relationships between commercial lenders and private borrowers are probably characterised by large differences of financial knowledge and expertise. It is an inherently unequal relationship. But it cannot have been Parliament's intention that the generality of such relationships should be liable to be reopened for that reason alone.*" [206]

5.34 Various factors which have been considered by the Courts under CCA 1974 s.140B were helpfully summarised in Deutsche Bank (Suisse) v Khan [2013] EWHC 482 (Comm), a case in which the mortgagors sought (unsuccessfully) to rely on s.140B in resisting claims for possession of 7 charged properties securing borrowing in excess of £50m which had been used to purchase the properties):

"*(1) In relation to the fairness of the terms themselves:*

a. whether the term is commonplace and/or in the nature of the product in question;

b. whether there are sound commercial reasons for the term;

c. whether it represents a legitimate and proportionate attempt by the creditor to protect its position;

d. to the extent that a term is solely for the benefit of the lender, whether it exists to protect him from a risk which the debtor does not face;

[206] Para 10.

e. *the scale of the lending and whether it was commercial or quasi-commercial in nature (a court is likely to be slower to find unfairness in high value lending arrangements between commercial parties than in credit agreements affecting consumers); and*

f. *the strength (or otherwise) of the debtors bargaining position;*

g. *whether the terms have been individually negotiated or are pro forma terms and, if so, whether they have been presented on a "take it or leave it" basis;*

(2) *In relation to the creditor's conduct before and at the time of formation:*

a. *whether the creditor applied any pressure on the borrowers to execute the agreement (if an agreement has been entered into with a sense of urgency it will be relevant to consider to what extent responsibility for this lay with the debtor, as distinct from the creditor);*

b. *whether the creditor understood and had reasonable grounds to believe that the borrower had experience of the relevant arrangements and had available to him the advice of solicitors;*

c. *whether the creditor had any reason to think that the debtor had not read or understood the terms; and*

d. *whether the debtor demurred at the time of formation over the terms he now suggests are unfair (this point has particular force if he did complain over other terms);*

(3) *In relation to the creditor's conduct following formation and leading up to enforcement:*

a. *whether any demand was prompted by an "improper motive" or was the consequence of an "arbitrary decision";*

b. *whether the creditor has shown patience and, before leaping to enforcement, has taken steps in the hope of reaching some form of accommodation (for example by attending meetings, engaging in correspondence and/or inviting proposals); and*

c. *whether the debtor has resisted attempts at accommodation by raising unfounded claims against the creditor."*[207]

5.35 If a mortgagor under a regulated mortgage contract, or home purchase plan, wishes to raise unfairness of contract terms, it will be necessary to rely on the Unfair Terms in Consumer Contracts Regulations 1999 (UTCCR 1999) or the Consumer Rights Act 2015 (CRA 2015) both of which apply to mortgages.[208] This is, again, a complicated area of law, a detailed consideration of which is outside the scope of this text, thus only a brief overview is provided below.

5.36 The UTCCR 1999 apply to a mortgage entered into between a seller or supplier – a person acting for purposes relating to his trade, business or profession – and a consumer – a natural person acting for purposes outside a trade, business or profession.[209] They do not apply to contractual terms which reflect mandatory statutory or regulatory provisions.[210] A contractual term which has not been individually negotiated shall be regarded as unfair if, "*contrary to the requirement of good faith, it causes a significant imbalance in the parties' rights and obligations arising under the contract, to the detriment of the*

[207] Para 346.

[208] See, (considering UTCCR 1999), *Evans v Cherry Tree Finance Ltd* [2008] EWCA Civ 331. UTCCR 1999 apply to any mortgage granted between 1 October 1999 and 30 September 2015. CRA 2015 applies to mortgages granted on or after 1 October 2015.

[209] Reg 4(1), read with the definitions in reg 3.

[210] Reg 4(2)(a).

consumer".[211] The fact that a term has been individually negotiated does not necessarily mean, however, that the UTCCR 2015 will not apply to the remainder of the contract, if an overall assessment of the agreement indicates that it is a pre-formulated standard contract.[212]

5.37 The fairness (or unfairness) of a contractual term is to be assessed taking into account the nature of the good or services for which the contract was concluded and by referring, at the time of the conclusion of the contract, to all the circumstances attending the conclusion of the contact and all the other terms of the contract or of another contract on which it is dependent.[213] The assessment of the fairness of a term does not apply to (a) the definition of the main subject matters of the contract – i.e. the essential obligations of the contract[214]; or (b) the adequacy of the price or remuneration in respect of the goods or services supplied, provided the relevant term(s) is in plain, intelligible language.[215] Schedule 2 contains a non-exhaustive list of terms which may be regarded as unfair. If a term is found to be unfair, then it is not enforceable against the consumer, but if the contract is capable of continuing in existence without that term then the contract shall continue to bind the parties.[216]

5.38 The CCA 2015 broadly reflects the UTCCR regime which it replaced with three key differences:

---

[211] Reg 5(1). The onus of establishing that a term has been individually negotiated rests with the seller or supplier who claims that it was: reg 5(4).

[212] Reg 5(3).

[213] Reg 6(1).

[214] (C-26/13) *Kasler v OTP Jelzalogbank Zrt* [2014] Bus. L.R. 664.

[215] Reg 6(2).

[216] Reg 8.

(i) Even terms that have been individually negotiated can be unenforceable if they are found to be unfair – cf the position under the UTCCR 1999[217];

(ii) A consumer is defined as an individual who is acting *wholly or mainly* outside the purposes of a trade, business, craft or profession[218]; and

(iii) A term may not be assessed for unfairness "*to the extent that (a) it specifies the main subject matter of the contract; or (b) the assessment is of the appropriateness of the price payable under the contract by comparison with the goods, digital content or services supplied under it*"[219] – provided that the term is transparent[220] and prominent.[221]

5.39 The test for unfairness is the same as that under the UTCCR 1999. As under the UTCCR 1999, an unfair term is not enforceable against the consumer,[222] but the contract continues to otherwise have effect, so far as practicable.[223]

Human Rights

5.40 In light of *McDonald v McDonald* [2017] A.C. 273, in which the Supreme Court held it was not open to a tenant to raise an Article 8 defence in a possession claim against a private landlord; and *Horsham Properties Group Ltd v Clark* [2009] 1 W.L.R.

[217] Cf the definition in CRA 2015 s.62 when compared with UTCCR 1991 reg 5(1).

[218] CRA 2015 s.2(3).

[219] CRA 2015 s.64.

[220] "*... expressed in plain and intelligible language*" and, for a term in a written document, legible: CRA 2015 s.64(3).

[221] "*... brought to the consumer's attention in such a way that an average consumer would be aware of the term*": CRA 2015 s.64(4).

[222] CRA 2015 s.62(1).

[223] CRA 2015 s.67.

1255, in which it was held that the sale of the property to the claimants by the mortgagee without first obtaining a court order for possession of the property did not violate the defendants' ECHR rights or provide a defence to the subsequent possession claim, it is unlikely that a mortgagor will be able to raise a successful ECHR defence in proceedings brought by a private mortgagee.[224] The Court of Appeal has also previously held that the power to grant relief pursuant to AJA 1970 and AJA 1973 s.8 are consistent with a mortgagor's ECHR rights.[225]

The Equality Act 2010

5.41 It would, in principle, be open to a mortgagor to raise a defence to a possession claim based on the Equality Act 2010. However, given the analysis of the Court of Appeal in *Green v Southern Pacific Mortgages Ltd* [2018] EWCA Civ 854, in which such a defence was acknowledged in principle but rejected on the facts, the circumstances which such a defence could be successfully advanced may be rather limited.

Counterclaims

5.42 A counterclaim will not usually provide a 'defence' to a claim for possession – in the sense of defeating the claim for possession of the property to be delivered up to the mortgagee – absent some unusual term in the mortgage agreement itself. In practice, however, where a claim for possession is brought on the grounds of arrears, and the counterclaim would provide a set-off of those arrears, that may provide grounds for the exercise of the Court's discretion under AJA 1970 s.36 and thus, in practice, prevent the mortgagee recovering possession of the property. This is discussed further in Chapter 7.

---

[224] Although it should be noted that in *Horsham Properties* Briggs J expressly left open the question of whether there might have been a violation of the defendants' rights under Article 1 of the 1st Protocol if the property had been sold before the right to exercise the power of sale under s.101 LPA 1925 had properly arisen.

[225] *Barclays Bank Plc v Alcorn* [2002] EWCA Civ 817.

CHAPTER SIX

OCCUPIERS AND THIRD PARTIES

Authorised tenants

6.1 Where a mortgage has been granted in order to fund the purchase of the property, it will usually be the case that the mortgage will take priority over any tenancy or other interest granted by the mortgagor, which will usually be granted subject to the rights and entitlements enjoyed by the mortgagee. Whilst LPA 1925 s.99(1) provides that a mortgagor in possession may grant leases binding on an incumbrancer (such as a mortgagee) that power will often be excluded in a mortgage agreement.

6.2 An authorised tenant who is in possession of the property may, however, be able to defend a claim for possession brought by the mortgagee if:

(i) The mortgage agreement does not exclude the right to grant tenancies of the property, the property has been let at or above market rate,[226] and if consent of the mortgagee is required under the mortgage that consent has been obtained[227];

(ii) The tenancy was granted before the mortgage was registered. This is more likely to arise where the mortgage is a second charge on the property; or

(iii) The mortgagee is essentially estopped from asserting that it is not bound by the tenancy because it has either

[226] LPA 1925 s.99(6).

[227] *Habib Bank AG Zurich v Utocroft 2 Limited* [2015] EWHC 3481 (Ch).

consented to the tenancy, or is taken to have acquiesced in the tenancy.[228]

6.3 In respect of that third situation, the mere fact that the lender knows of an unauthorised tenancy but does not take any steps to evict the tenant is not sufficient.[229]

6.4 As set out in para 3.11 above, where a mortgagee knows that a tenant is in occupation of the property,[230] that person should be named as a defendant to the proceedings and must, in any event, be served with notice of the proposed hearing as the occupier of the property.[231] Where the tenancy is binding as against the mortgagee, that would in principle provide a defence to the claim for possession, at least as against the tenant. At the first hearing of the possession claim where the property is occupied by an authorised tenant, the court will therefore consider whether further directions are required, whether the claim should be adjourned until possession has been recovered against the tenant (for example, through the mortgagor or a receiver terminating any tenancy and seeking possession if not provided voluntarily) or to make an order for possession conditional upon the tenant's right of occupation.[232]

Unauthorised tenants

6.5 An unauthorised tenancy (i.e. one granted in breach of the mortgage conditions) or tenancy which is not otherwise binding on the mortgagee will not provide a defence to a possession claim, although the tenant should still be joined as a defendant or at

---

[228] *Parker v Braithwaite* [1952] 2 All E.R. 837.

[229] *Taylor v Ellis* [1960] Ch 368.

[230] The mortgagee should, in any event, make specific inquiries in that respect prior to commencing the claim where the claim is a residential property: see para 4.10 above.

[231] See para 3.9 above.

[232] Para 7.2 of the Pre Action Protocol.

least served with the notice of the hearing of the possession claim. The fact that a tenancy may be subject to statutory protection, for example under the Rent Act 1977 or Housing Act 1988, does not make it binding on the mortgagee if it would otherwise be unauthorised.

6.6 Whilst the existence of the unauthorised tenancy will not provide a defence to the possession proceedings, an unauthorised tenant who is within the contractual period of a tenancy is a person with an interest in the equity of redemption and who could, therefore, pay off the mortgage debt and take a transfer of the mortgage.[233]

6.7 An unauthorised tenant cannot ask the court to exercise its discretion under AJA 1970 s.36[234] but some protection was introduced in October 2010 when the Mortgage Repossessions (Protection of Tenants etc) Act 2010 (MRPTA 2010) and the Dwelling House (Execution of Possession Orders by Mortgagees) Regulations 2010 (DHR 2010) came into force.

6.8 Pursuant to MRPTA 2010, where a mortgagee seeks possession of a dwellinghouse which is occupied by an unauthorised tenant, the tenant can apply for a stay of execution of the possession order of up to two months. Such application can be made by the tenant as a defendant in the proceedings,[235] or following the making of the order but prior to its execution.[236]

6.9 MRPTA 2010 s.2 precludes a mortgagee from executing a possession order unless he has given notice at the property of the "prescribed step taken for the purpose of execution" and only after the end of the "prescribed period" beginning with the day

---

233 *Tarn v Turner* (1888) 39 Ch.D 456 discussed in *Britannia Building Society v Earl* [1990] 1 W.L.R. 422.

234 *Britannia Building Society v Earl* [1990] 1 W.L.R. 422.

235 MRPTA 2010 s.1(2).

236 MRPTA 2010 s.1(4).

on which notice is given.[237] The "prescribed step" is the mortgagee making an application to the court for a warrant for possession of the property,[238] and the "prescribed period" is 14 days.[239] The notice should be given in the prescribed form, set out in the Schedule to the DHR 2010, and should be given to the tenant by:

(i) Sending the notice to the property by first class or registered post in an envelope addressed to the tenant by name (if known) or, if not, to "The Tenant or Occupier";

(ii) By leaving the notice at the property (i) in an envelope addressed to the tenant by name (if known) or, if not, to "the Tenant or Occupier", or affixed to and displayed in a prominent place where its contents can be read by a person entering the property; or

(iii) By personal service upon a person who appears to be in residence at the property.[240]

6.10 Where an application is made under MRPTA 2010 s.1(4) (i.e. after the order for possession has been made), the conditions set out in s.1(4) must be satisfied, namely:

(i) The court did not exercise its powers under s.1(2) when making the order or, if it did, the applicant was not the tenant when it exercised those powers;

(ii) The applicant has asked the mortgagee to give an undertaking in writing not to enforce the order for two

---

[237] MRPTA 2010 s.2(2).

[238] DHR 2010 reg 2.

[239] DHR 2010 reg 3.

[240] DHR 2010 reg 4.

months beginning with the date the undertaking is given; and

(iii) The mortgagee has not given such an undertaking.

6.11 The power under MRPTA 2010 s.1 may only be exercised once (the court cannot exercise the power under s.1(4) if it has already exercised the power under s.1(2)) and it appears that only one stay will be granted, so multiple applications cannot be made individually by joint tenants of the property.[241]

6.12 The court may order a stay, or suspension, for a period not exceeding two months: it is not an automatic two month grace period. In determining the period for which the stay or suspension is to be granted, the court must have regard to:

(i) The circumstances of the tenant; and

(ii) If there is an outstanding breach by the tenant of a term of the unauthorised tenancy –

  (i) the nature of that breach; and

  (ii) whether the tenant might reasonably be expected to have avoided breaching that term or to have remedied the breach.

6.13 The court may make any postponement, stay or suspension conditional on the making of payments to the mortgagee in respect of the occupation of the property. That will not create a new tenancy as between the mortgagee and unauthorised tenant.[242]

---

[241] i.e. applications by different tenants at different times will not result in multiple stays, or extensions of the 2 month period. See MRPTA 2010 s.1(9) and para 10.7 of the Communities and Local Government Guidance to the Mortgage Repossession (Protection of Tenants etc) Act 2010.

[242] MRPTA 2010 s.1(6).

Spouses, civil partners and cohabitees

6.14 As discussed in Chapter 4, "home rights"[243] do not confer on spouse or civil partner B any greater right to occupy the property against a mortgagee than are enjoyed by spouse or civil partner A,[244] unless their rights are a charge affecting the mortgagee on the estate or interest charged.[245] Similarly, former spouses or civil partners, who may enjoy similar rights to occupy the property at issue pursuant to an order made under FLA 1996 ss.35 or 36 do not enjoy any greater right to occupy the property against a mortgagee than are enjoyed by their former spouse or civil partner.[246]

6.15 However, where a claim for possession of the property is commenced, a spouse, former spouse, civil partner, former civil partner, co-habitant or former co-habitant may apply to be joined as a defendant under FLA 1996 s.55 and may, in practice, be able to prevent the mortgagee obtaining possession of the property if they can satisfy the court that they can pay any sums due under the mortgage, and the court is satisfied that it should exercise its jurisdiction under AJA 1970 s.36 to either adjourn the proceedings, or to stay or suspend execution of any possession order on terms.

Overriding interests

6.16 A claim for possession may also be defeated if if a claim to an overriding interest is successfully made by an occupier of the property. An overriding interest is defined in LRA 2002 Schedule 3 para 2 as:

---

[243] Under the FLA 1996, or their predecessor provisions

[244] FLA 1996 s.54(3).

[245] FLA 1996 s.54(4).

[246] FLA 1996 s.54(3).

"An interest belonging at the time of the disposition to a person in actual occupation, so far as relating to land, of which he is in actual occupation, except for –

(a) An interest under a settlement under the Settled Land Act 1925 (c18);

(b) An interest of a person of whom inquiry was made before the disposition and who failed to disclose the right when he could have and could reasonably have been expected to do so;

(c) An interest –

 (i) Which belongs to a person whose occupation would not have been obvious on a reasonably careful inspection of the land at the time of the disposition; and

 (ii) Of which the person to whom the disposition is made does not have actual knowledge at that time;

(d) A leasehold estate in land granted to take effect in possession after the end of the period of three months beginning with the date of the grant and which has not taken effect in possession at the time of the disposition."

6.17 The interest must be a proprietary right (a purely contractual right such as a licence is not sufficient). In the mortgage context, this is likely to take the form of a beneficial interest under a trust, a proprietary estoppel or a 'mere equity',[247] such as a right of rectification or right to rescind for fraud. The person claiming the overriding interest must be in actual occupation of the property (a legal entitlement to occupy is not sufficient) and

[247] An equity by estoppel or mere equity has effect from the time the equity arises as an interest capable of binding successors in title : LRA 2002 s.116.

that occupation must be obvious on a reasonably careful inspection of the land at the date the mortgage is entered into.[248]

6.18 In respect of unregistered land, a mortgagee will be bound by any equitable interest of which he had actual, imputed or constructive knowledge,[249] unless that interest has been overreached as provided for by LPA 1925 s.2. In practice, this is likely to be the case where a mortgage has been granted by two legal owner trustees and the capital monies paid to them.[250]

---

[248] See, for example, *Thompson v Foy* [2010] 1 P. & C.R. 16.

[249] LPA 1925 s.196.

[250] See, for example, *City of London Building Society v Flegg* [1988] A.C. 54.

CHAPTER SEVEN

MONEY CLAIMS AND COUNTERCLAIMS

7.1 As discussed in Chapter 1, a mortgagee has a number of avenues which he can pursue when the mortgagor falls into arrears, or otherwise breaches the mortgage. Where a claim for possession of mortgaged property is pursued, it will often include a claim for monies due, based on the mortgagor's personal covenant to pay.

Monies due under the mortgage

7.2 Prescribed form N120 (Particulars of claim for possession (mortgaged residential premises)) provides for the mortgagee to set out the details of monies due and owing at the date of the claim, including any agreed repayments of loan and interest which are in arrears, the total amount to pay off the mortgage in full at a date not more than 14 days after issue, and any additional payments required under the terms of the mortgage.[251]

7.3 Where the claim includes a claim on the personal covenant to pay and a possession order is made, the order will usually provide for the mortgagor to pay off the mortgage in full. If the court makes a suspended order for possession, then the obligation to pay off that sum will usually also be suspended on the same terms.[252] Where a possession order is sought against a third party in possession, a claim on the personal covenant to pay can only be pleaded as against the mortgagor(s), and care

[251] See also the general requirements in Practice Direction 55A discussed at para 3.7 above.

[252] See Chapter 9.

will need to be taken to ensure that the standard form is properly amended to reflect that position.

7.4 As the money claim is based on the personal covenant to pay, care must be taken when the claim is based on an 'all monies' clause. As discussed in Chapter 5 above,[253] if arrears are relied on, or a debt pursued, when seeking possession of one property securing such a charge, that is likely to prevent the same arrears being relied on, or a money claim for all monies due being pursued, in a separate claim for possession of a second property.

7.5 Similarly, if the mortgagor is insolvent, or insolvency is imminent, restrictions may apply to any claim which includes a claim on the personal covenant to pay. This is discussed further in Chapter 8.

Counterclaims

7.6 As discussed in Chapter 5 above, a counterclaim will rarely provide a 'defence' to a claim for possession, but it may be material to the court's discretion to suspend an order under AJA 1970 s.36 and provide a set-off against any money judgment made against the mortgagor. If, however, the counter-claim is for a sum that would exceed the amount secured by the mortgage, then the mortgagor should include a claim for redemption of the mortgage within the counterclaim, although that would need to be pursued swiftly to ensure that redemption of the mortgage could occur before the proceedings for possession concluded.

7.7 Potential defences to a possession claim, some of which might also give rise to a counter-claim by the mortgagor, are discussed more generally in Chapter 5. A mortgagor under a regulated mortgage agreement might, however, also be able to make a claim for damages if the mortgagee has acted in breach of rules prescribed by the Financial Services Authority pursuant to its

---

[253] See para 5.25

powers in FSMA 2000 Part 9A Chapter 1, and if the mortgagor has suffered loss as a result.[254] The mortgagor may only bring such a claim where the breach has caused him financial loss, so it most likely to arise in connection with the mortgagee's actions or omissions when the mortgage was being considered or entered into. The key rules are likely to be those contained in the Mortgages and Home Finance: Conduct of Business Sourcebook.[255] It is important to distinguish between rules (marked 'R') and guidance (marked 'G') as it is only breach of the rules which may give rise to a potential claim in damages. Breach of the rules does not, however, render the transaction void and unenforceable,[256] and would not, therefore provide a defence to a claim for possession of the property as would be the case if the mortgage had been entered into in breach of the 'general prohibition' in FSMA 2000.[257]

Costs

7.8 Where a claim is made for possession of the property, it is not necessary for the mortgagee to claim the costs associated with the claim as they will ordinarily be added to the security pursuant to the mortgagee's equitable right to obtain reimbursement from the security of costs reasonably and properly incurred in enforcing or preserving his security.[258] That equitable right may, although does not need to be, reinforced by any express provision in the mortgage agreement, although such provision may be necessary if the mortgagee wishes to recover its costs on an indemnity basis.[259] Whilst

[254] FSMA 2000 s.138D(2).

[255] Available on the FCA's website at www.handbook.fca.org.uk at the date of writing.

[256] *Thakker v Northern Rock (Asset Management) Plc* [2014] EWHC 2107.

[257] See paras 5.3 – 5.6 above.

[258] *Parker-Tweedale v Dunbar Bank Plc & ors (No 2)* [1991] Ch 26 per Nourse L.J. at pg 33.

[259] See *Helden v Strathmore Ltd* [2011] H.L.R. 41.

Form N120 does not include a claim for costs in the prayer, the prescribed form of order for both an immediate (N26) and a suspended possession order (N31) provides for the claimant's costs to be added to the amount owing under the mortgage.

7.9 That does not mean, however, that the court's ordinary powers and discretions with regard to costs do not apply. The court retains its discretion to award costs in either party's favour. The usual rule is that the successful party will pay the unsuccessful party's costs,[260] but having regard to all the circumstances of the case, such as the parties' conduct[261] – including conduct before proceedings commence[262] – the court may make a different order.[263] A court may disallow a mortgagee's costs if it considers appropriate, but if the mortgagee is not to be permitted to add the costs to his security this should be expressly addressed, as a costs order against a mortgagee will not be sufficient in and of itself to disapply the mortgagee's general equitable or contractual entitlement.[264]

The Debt Respite Scheme moratorium

7.10 In November 2020, the Debt Respite Scheme (Breathing Space Moratorium and Mental Health Crisis Moratorium) (England and Wales) Regulations 2020 (DRSR 2020) came into force. The DRSR 2020 provide for the first part of a wider Government initiative to assist people in 'problem debt' and, in broad terms, they are intended to provide certain protections to those in such debt from their creditors. The DRSR 2020 provide for two types of moratorium: a "breathing space

[260] CPR r.44.2(2)(a).

[261] CPR r.44.2(4).

[262] CPR r.44.2(5). This may be particularly relevant if the mortgagee has failed to comply with the Pre-Action Protocol.

[263] CPR r.44.2(2)(b).

[264] *Parker-Tweedale v Dunbar Bank Plc & ors (No 2)* [1991] Ch 26.

moratorium"[265] and a "mental health crisis moratorium".[266] Where either moratorium applies, this is likely to have implications for (i) the mortgagee's ability to recover any interest, fees, penalties or charges arising in respect of mortgage arrears during the moratorium period; (ii) the commencement or prosecution of any proposed or extant proceedings; and (iii) the enforcement of any court order which may already have been obtained.

7.11 In order to benefit from a breathing space moratorium, the debtor must apply to a debt advice provider from whom he has already sought advice as to the suitability, conditions and consequences of a breathing space moratorium.[267] The application must include details of the debts to which the debtor is subject at the date of the application, contact details of any creditors to whom each debt is owned, and details of any enforcement agent or other agent instructed by a creditor for the purpose of collection or enforcement of the debt including the agent's contact details.[268] The debt advice provider must initiate a breathing space moratorium if the debt advice provider considers that the debtor meets the eligibility criteria in reg 24(3),[269] the conditions in reg 24(4) are met, and the debts to be included in the moratorium are "qualifying debts". Mortgage arrears (although not the principal sum) are qualifying debts under the DRSR 2020, as are amounts which

---

265 DRSR 2020 Part 2.

266 DRSR 2020 Part 3.

267 Reg 23. On debt advice providers, see reg 3.

268 Reg 23(5).

269 The debtor is an individual, who owes a qualifying debt to a creditor, is domiciled or ordinarily resident in England or Wales, is not subject to a debt relief order, is not subject to an interim or individual voluntary arrangement, is not an undischarged bankrupt, is not subject to another breathing space moratorium or if previously subject to a breathing space moratorium that moratorium ended more than 12 months before the date of the application, and is not subject to a mental health crisis moratorium.

the debtor is liable to pay under or in relation to an order or warrant for possession of the debtor's place of residence or business or a court judgment.[270] The conditions in reg 24(4) are that, in light of the information provided by the debtor and any other information obtained by the debt advice provider, (a) the debtor is unable, or is unlikely to be able to repay some or all of their debt as it falls due, and (b) a breathing space moratorium would be appropriate.[271] A breathing space moratorium is initiated upon the Secretary of State, having received the required information from the debt advice provider, causing an entry to be made on the register maintained by the Secretary of State for that purpose[272] and sending notification to the creditors and agents whose details have been provided.[273] A breathing space moratorium will usually last for 60 days unless the debtor dies, or the moratorium is cancelled under reg 18 (review and cancellation as a result of a creditor request), reg 19 (court application by creditor for cancellation of the moratorium) or reg 27 (midway review).[274]

7.12 An application for a mental health crisis moratorium may be made by or on behalf of[275] a debtor, in circumstances where the debtor is receiving mental health crisis treatment.[276] The application must be supported by evidence from an approved mental health professional[277] (as well as such information as can

[270] Reg 5.

[271] Which is to be considered having regard to the matters set out in reg 24(5).

[272] See reg 35.

[273] Reg 22.

[274] Reg 26.

[275] Reg 29(1).

[276] As defined in reg 28(2).

[277] Reg 29(2)-(3).

be provided in respect of the debtor's debts and creditors[278]). The conditions for making a mental health crisis moratorium are similar to those for a breathing space moratorium (with the debt advice provider also obtaining information relevant to the debtor's financial standing from at least one credit reference agency,[279] and being satisfied that an approved mental health professional has provided evidence that the debtor is receiving mental health crisis treatment[280]) but, if made, will not end until the earliest of (a) the end of the period of 30 days beginning with which the debtor stops receiving mental health crisis treatment; (b) the end of the period of 30 days beginning with the day on which the debt advice provider makes a request for information to the debtor's nominated contact regarding the debtor's continued (or concluded) mental health crisis treatment and does not receive a response; (c) the cancellation of the mental health crisis moratorium under regs 18, 19 or 34[281]; or (d) the day on which it ends under the terms of reg 21 as a result of the death of the debtor.[282]

7.13 The effect of a breathing space moratorium or a mental health crisis moratorium is to prevent a creditor taking any specified steps in relation to any moratorium debt[283] during the moratorium period unless permission has been granted by the

---

278 Reg 29(4).

279 Reg 29(1).

280 Reg 29(4).

281 Cancellation of the mental health crisis moratorium where the debt advice provider considers that the evidence from the mental health professional contains inaccurate, misleading or fraudulent information, or the debtor requests that the debt advice provider cancels the moratorium.

282 Reg 32.

283 Defined in reg 5 as any qualifying debt – (a) that was incurred by a debtor in relation to whom a moratorium is in place (b) that was owned by the debtor at the point when the application for the moratorium was made and (c) about which information has been provided to the Secretary of State by a debt advice provider under the DRSR 2020.

county court or other court or tribunal where legal proceedings concerning the debt have been or could be issued or started, or unless otherwise provided for by the DRSR 2020. The specified steps are taking any steps to:

(i) require a debtor to pay interest that accrues on a moratorium debt during a moratorium period;

(ii) require a debtor to pay fees, penalties or charges in relation to a moratorium debt that accrues during a moratorium period;

(iii) take any enforcement action in respect of a moratorium debt (whether the right to take such action arises under a contract, by virtue of an enactment or otherwise); or

(iv) instruct an agent to take any of those steps.[284]

7.14 A creditor or agent takes enforcement action if (inter alia) they:

(i) take a step to collect a moratorium debt from a debtor (this only applies to interest that accrues on any arrears on the debt where the moratorium debt is a secured debt[285]);

(ii) take a step to enforce a judgment or order issued by a court or tribunal before or during a moratorium period regarding a moratorium debt;

(iii) enforce security held in respect of a moratorium debt;

(iv) obtain a warrant;

[284] Reg 7(6)(a)-(6). A court may not give permission for a creditor or agent to take any of the steps specified in reg 7(6)(a)-(b): reg 7(3).

[285] Reg 7(9).

(v) (subject to regulation 12(4)(d)) sell or take control of a debtor's property or goods;

(vi) start any action or legal proceedings against a debtor relating to or as a consequence of non-payment of a moratorium debt,

(vii) make an application for default judgment in respect of a claim for money against the debtor.[286]

7.15 After the end of the moratorium period, neither a creditor nor their agent is entitled to:

(i) require a debtor to pay interest, fees, penalties or charges referred to in reg 7(6)(a) and (b) that accrued during the moratorium period; or

(ii) treat the non-payment of such interest, fees, penalties or charges as a default by the debtor under, or breach of the agreement between, the debtor and creditor.[287]

7.16 Any action taken in contravention of reg 7 is null and void.[288]

---

[286] Reg 7(7).

[287] Reg 7(10).

[288] Reg 7(12).

CHAPTER EIGHT

INSOLVENCY

8.1 This Chapter sets out an overview of the various insolvency regimes, and briefly discusses how they may affect a claim for possession of mortgaged property.[289]

Personal Insolvency – Bankruptcy

8.2 There are 4 circumstances in which an individual may become bankrupt:

(i) presentation of a petition by the debtor himself;

(ii) presentation of a petition (following service of a statutory demand) by a creditor who is owed more than £750 and does not hold security for the entirety of his debt;

(iii) presentation of a petition by the supervisor of a voluntary arrangement (IVA), in event of non-compliance with the terms of an IVA; or

(iv) presentation of a petition by a person who is bound, for the time being, by the terms of an IVA in the event of non-compliance with the terms of the same.

8.3 Bankruptcy is governed by Part IX of the Insolvency Act 1986 ("IA 1986").

[289] A detailed account of the various insolvency regimes and how they may affect the various rights and remedies of a mortgagee is outside the scope of this book, and where such issues may arise in a particular claim, it would be advisable to consult one of the more specialist insolvency texts.

8.4 The most important provision[290] in the context of an existing or pending action in relation to mortgaged property is s.285, which provides for a moratorium on legal proceedings against a bankrupt or his estate whilst a bankruptcy is pending or extant:

285.— Restriction on proceedings and remedies.

(1) At any time when proceedings on a bankruptcy application are ongoing or proceedings on a bankruptcy petition are pending or an individual has been made bankrupt the court may stay any action, execution or other legal process against the property or person of the debtor or, as the case may be, of the bankrupt.

(2) Any court in which proceedings are pending against any individual may, on proof that a bankruptcy application has been made or a bankruptcy petition has been presented in respect of that individual or that he is an undischarged bankrupt, either stay the proceedings or allow them to continue on such terms as it thinks fit.

(3) After the making of a bankruptcy order no person who is a creditor of the bankrupt in respect of a debt provable in the bankruptcy shall—

[290] Although see also IA 1986 ss.283 & 283A which concern the bankrupt's estate. S.283(1) provides that, subject to the exceptions / qualifications which follow, a bankrupt's estate for the purposes of the Act comprises all property belonging to or vesting in the bankrupt at the commencement of the bankruptcy and any property which, by reason of the Act, is comprised in that estate or treated as such. S.283(5) makes clear that such property remains subject to the rights of any other person, whether as a secured creditor or otherwise, unless the conditions in s.283(5)(a) or (b) are met. S.283A makes specific provision in relation to a property which, at the date of the bankruptcy, was the sole or principal residence of the bankrupt, his spouse or civil partner, or that of a former spouse or civil partner.

(a) have any remedy against the property or person of the bankrupt in respect of that debt, or

(b) before the discharge of the bankrupt, commence any action or other legal proceedings against the bankrupt except with the leave of the court and on such terms as the court may impose.

This is subject to section 346 (enforcement procedures) and 347 (limited right todistress).

(4) Subject as follows, subsection (3) does not affect the right of a secured creditor of the bankrupt to enforce his security.

(5) Where any goods of an undischarged bankrupt are held by any person by way of pledge, pawn or other security, the official receiver may, after giving notice in writing of his intention to do so, inspect the goods.

Where such a notice has been given to any person, that person is not entitled, without leave of the court, to realise his security unless he has given the trustee of the bankrupt's estate a reasonable opportunity of inspecting the goods and of exercising the bankrupt's right of redemption.

(6) References in this section to the property or goods of the bankrupt are to any of his property or goods, whether or not comprised in his estate.

8.5 There are two aspects to that moratorium which are potentially relevant to mortgage possession claims. The first, is the general power in IA 1986 s.285(1) and (2) for the court to stay proceedings when a bankruptcy application is ongoing or bankruptcy petition pending. The second, is the restriction on remedies in s.285(3) when an individual has been made bankrupt.

8.6 Any court may exercise the stay power in s.285(2) on proof that a bankruptcy petition is pending: *Re Eileen Davies* [1997] B.P.I.R. 619. However, for the purposes of s.285(3), "the court" means the court seized of the bankruptcy proceedings.

8.7 The moratorium in s.285(3) does not, however, affect the right of a mortgagee to enforce his security: see IA 1986 s.285(4).

8.8 In practice, this appears to mean that a mortgagee may bring proceedings for possession of the mortgaged property, but not sue on the personal obligation to pay the mortgage debt, without falling foul of the prohibition in IA 1986 s.285(3). In line with the reasoning in *Places for People Homes Ltd v Sharples* [2012] Ch 382, in which the Court of Appeal had to consider whether possession orders made against assured tenants who were bankrupt and subject to a debt relief order respectively had been made in breach of s.285(3), it appears that proceedings for possession should not normally be stayed under s.285(1), but again subject to the restriction where a money claim is also pursued.[291]

8.9 In respect of the requirement for leave, which would apply where a mortgagee sought to bring a money claim after the mortgagor had been made bankrupt,[292] there is some conflict of authority regarding the prohibition on commencing

[291] In *Sharples*, the Court of Appeal considered that the moratorium in s.285(3) was not engaged because the claim for possession, albeit on grounds of rent arrears, was not a "*remedy against the property...in respect of the debt*" within the meaning of s.285(3)(a), an order for possession rather being a remedy which restored the landlord to his "*full proprietary rights*" (see para 63). Whilst the parallels are not exact, and possession is often referred to as one of the remedies available to a mortgagee to enforce its security (although there is some conflict in the various commentaries as to whether a claim for vacant possession of land is, in fact, an action to enforce a mortgagee's security or merely a claim for recovery of land) it would seem somewhat strange if an unsecured creditor landlord was in a better position than a secured creditor mortgagee, given the terms of s.285.

[292] Although this would need to be for debts which could not have been proved in the bankruptcy.

proceedings without the permission of the court contained in s.285(3). One view which has been adopted is that the provision should be construed purposively, and that permission can be granted after proceedings are commenced, thus making good the failure to do so prior to issue: this was the approach adopted in *Bristol & West Building Society v Saunders* [1997] B.C.C. 83.

8.10 This approach was not, however, followed in *Re Taylor* [2007] Ch 50, in which H.H.J Kershaw considered that the grant of permission was a condition precedent to the court's jurisdiction to determine the substantive matter before it, and thus proceedings instituted without leave were void as against the bankrupt individual. This approach was thought to be consistent with the majority approach in *Seal v Chief Constable of South Wales Police* [2007] 1 W.L.R. 1859, considering the issue in civil proceedings in general.

8.11 *Re Taylor* was not, however, followed in *Bank of Ireland v Colliers International UK Plc (In Administration)* [2013] 2 W.L.R. 895 which considered a number of the formerly conflicting authorities, including *Saunders* and *Re Taylor*, concluding that *Saunders* approach was correct.[4] This would now seem to be the preferred approach – at least unless and until there is higher judicial consideration to the contrary.

Personal Insolvency – Individual Voluntary Arrangements

8.12 Individual voluntary arrangements are governed by IA 1986 Part VIII and are, in effect, a statutory compromise between a debtor and his creditors.

8.13 Prior to the implementation of the Insolvency Act 2000, it was a pre-requisite that the debtor obtain an interim order before putting a proposal to his creditors. Instead, there is a now an option to apply for an interim order, and the court will only grant the same if it is satisfied that:

(i) the debtor intends to make a proposal to his creditors for an IVA;

(ii) on the day of making the application the debtor was an undischarged bankrupt orwas able to petition for his own bankruptcy;

(iii) no previous application had been made by the debtor for an interim order in theperiod of 12 months ending with that day; and

(iv) the nominee under the debtor's proposal (ie the individual nominated to supervisethe IVA) is willing to act in relation to that proposal.[293]

8.14 IA 1986 s.254 makes provision for a court to take steps to protect the debtor's assets from legal action where an application for an interim order is pending:

"**254.— Effect of application.**

(1) At any time when an application under section 253 for an interim order is pending,

(a) no landlord or other person to whom rent is payable may exercise any right of forfeiture by peaceable re-entry in relation to premises let to the debtor in respectof a failure by the debtor to comply with any term or condition of his tenancy ofsuch premises, except with the leave of the court, and

(b) the court may forbid the levying of any distress on the debtor's property or its subsequent sale, or both, and stay any action, execution or other

[293] IA 1986 s.255(1).

legal process against the property or person of the debtor.

(2) Any court in which proceedings are pending against an individual may, on proof that an application under that section has been made in respect of that individual, either stay the proceedings or allow them to continue on such terms as it thinks fit"

8.15 S.252 provides for a moratorium on legal proceedings against the debtor where an interim order is made by the court, in the following terms:

"**252.— Interim order of court.**

(1) In the circumstances specified below, the court may in the case of a debtor (being anindividual) make an interim order under this section.

(2) An interim order has the effect that, during the period for which it is in force—

(a) no bankruptcy petition relating to the debtor may be presented or proceededwith,

(aa) no landlord or other person to whom rent is payable may exercise any right of forfeiture by peaceable re-entry in relation to premises let to the debtor in respectof a failure by the debtor to comply with any term or condition of his tenancy ofsuch premises, except with the leave of the court, and

(b) no other proceedings, and no execution or other legal process, may be commenced or continued and no distress may be levied against the debtor or his property except with the leave of the court"

8.16 The interim moratorium is broad in its terms – *no other proceedings .... or legal process"* may be commenced or continued without the leave of the court.

8.17 There seems no reason to believe that the moratorium under Part VIII would be construed any differently to that in Part IX (bankruptcy), such that if leave were not sought before commencing proceedings, those proceedings would be invalid. Once an interim order is in place, therefore, a mortgagee will be unable to commence, or continue, any ongoing proceedings, or to enforce any judgment it may previously have obtained, without the leave of the court.

8.18 There is no similar statutory moratorium which applies once the IVA has been approved. The debtor's creditors may not, however, approve any proposal or modification which "*affects the right of a secured creditor of the debtor to enforce his security, except with the concurrence of the creditor concerned*".[294] A mortgagee is not therefore affected by an IVA (or CVA) unless he expressly agrees to be so bound.[295] Thus, whilst he is precluded from enforcing his security whilst the interim order is in force, the mortgagee may rely on the rights and remedies he otherwise enjoyed to enforce his security unless, on a proper construction of the IVA, he consents to those being restricted under its terms.[296]

Personal Insolvency – Debt Relief Orders ("DROs")

8.19 DROs were introduced by the Tribunals, Courts and Enforcement Act 2007, which inserted a new Part 7A and Schedule 4ZA into the IA 1986 with effect from 6 April

---

[294] IA 10986 s.258 IA 1986 (IVA), s.4 (CVA).

[295] See *Khan v. Permayer* [2001] B.P.I.R. 95 (CA) at para 19.

[296] *Whitehead v Household Mortgage Corp Plc* [2003] 1 W.L.R. 1173 (CA) at para 19.

2009.[297] They broadly reflect the bankruptcy order regime, without payment of the higher fees which apply in that regime. The effect of the order is to stay enforcement of debts by creditors, with the debts discharged after a specified period (one year). Given the financial limits that apply, it is perhaps unlikely that these would arise in the context of mortgaged residential property, but a brief overview is set out below for completeness.

8.20 The main elements of the DRO regime are, in summary:

(i) an individual who is unable to pay his debts may apply for a DRO in respect of hisqualifying debts (s.251A(1));

(ii) to qualify as a qualifying debt, the debt must be for a liquidated sum (s.251A(2));

(iii) the applicant must not have been the subject of a DRO in the previous 6 years (Sch 4ZA para 5);

(iv) the applicant's debt must not exceed the prescribed amount (Sch 4ZA para 6) –currently £30,000;

(v) the applicant's monthly surplus income[298] must not exceed the prescribed amount(Sch 4ZA para 7) – currently £75;

(vi) the value of the applicant's assets must not exceed the prescribed amount (Sch 4ZA para 8) – currently £2000;

(vii) the application is made, via an "approved intermediary", to the official receiver (s.251B(1)), and

[297] There is a helpful summary of the purpose and effect of DROs in *Secretary of State for Work and Pensions v Payne & Cooper* [2011] 1 W.L.R. 1723 at paras 14-15.

[298] After paying tax, national insurance, and normal household expenses.

must include a list of the debts to which the applicant is subject at the date of the application (s.251B(2));

(viii) when the DRO is made, it must include a list of the debts which the official receiver is satisfied were qualifying debts at the date of the application date, specifying the amount of the debt at that time and the creditor to whom it was owed (s.251E(3));

(ix) a creditor specified in a DRO may object to the making of the order or the inclusion of the debt in the list of qualifying debts (s.251K).

8.21 When a DRO is made, a moratorium is imposed by virtue of s.251G which provides asfollows:

"**251G Moratorium from qualifying debts**

(1) A moratorium commences on the effective date for a debt relief order in relation to each qualifying debt specified in the order ("a specified qualifying debt").

(2) During the moratorium, the creditor to whom a specified qualifying debt is owed–

(a) has no remedy in respect of the debt, and

(b) may not–

(i) commence a creditor's petition in respect of the debt, or

(ii) otherwise commence any action or other legal proceedings against thedebtor for the debt,

except with the permission of the court and on such terms as the court may impose.

(3) If on the effective date a creditor to whom a specified qualifying debt is owed has any such petition, action or other proceeding as mentioned in subsection (2)(b) pendingin any court, the court may–

(a) stay the proceedings on the petition, action or other proceedings (as the casemay be), or

(b) allow them to continue on such terms as the court thinks fit.

(4) In subsection (2)(a) and (b) references to the debt include a reference to any interest, penalty or other sum that becomes payable in relation to that debt after the application date.

(5) Nothing in this section affects the right of a secured creditor of the debtor to enforcehis security."

8.22 As discussed at para 8.8 above, this moratorium would not appear to affect a mortgagee's ability to seek possession of the mortgaged property, although would likely affect any money claim that might be made.

Company Insolvency – Administration

8.23 The administration regime was comprehensively overhauled by the Enterprise Act 2002, with the reforms set out in IA 1986 Sch B1.

8.24 There are three routes by which a company may be put into administration. A company enters administration on the appointment of an administrator:

(i) By an administration order of the court under Sch B1 para 10;

(ii) By the holder of a floating charge under Sch B1 para 14;

(iii) By the company or its directors under Sch B1 para 22.

8.25 Whatever route is adopted, the administrator is required to perform his functions with the aim of achieving one of the objectives set out in para 3 of Sch B1, which objectives are hierarchical:

(i) Rescuing the company as a going concern; or

(ii) Achieving a better result for the company's creditors as a whole than would be likely if the company were wound up (without first being in administration); or

(iii) Realising property in order to make a distribution to one or more secured creditors.

8.26 The moratorium on legal process whilst a company is in administration is set out in IA 1986 of Sch B1 para 43 of the Act:

"(1) This paragraph applies to a company in administration.

(2) No step may be taken to enforce security over the company's property except—

(a) with the consent of the administrator, or

(b) with the permission of the court.

(3) No step may be taken to repossess goods in the company's possession under a hire-purchase agreement except—

(a) with the consent of the administrator, or

(b) with the permission of the court.

(4) A landlord may not exercise a right of forfeiture by peaceable re-entry in relation to premises let to the company except—

(a) with the consent of the administrator, or

(b) with the permission of the court.

(5) In Scotland, a landlord may not exercise a right of irritancy in relation to premises let to the company except—

(a) with the consent of the administrator, or

(b) with the permission of the court.

(6) No legal process (including legal proceedings, execution, distress and diligence) maybe instituted or continued against the company or property of the company except—

(a) with the consent of the administrator, or

(b) with the permission of the court.

(6A) An administrative receiver of the company may not be appointed.

(7) Where the court gives permission for a transaction under this paragraph it mayimpose a condition on or a requirement in connection with the transaction.

(8) In this paragraph "landlord" includes a person to whom rent is payable"

8.27 Sch B1 Para 44 makes provision for an interim moratorium, applying the moratorium on insolvency proceedings (Sch B1 para 42) and other legal proceedings (Sch B1 para 43) to the period where the process to put the company into administration has been commenced but not yet completed or taken effect. It is somewhat controversial.

8.28 In terms of when the court's permission will be granted for proceedings caught by para 43, the seminal guidance is that set out in the judgment of Nicholls LJ in *Re Atlantic Computer Systems Plc* [1992] Ch 505. Where granting permission is unlikely to be impede the achievement of the purpose for which the administration order was made, permission is likely to be granted. In other cases, the court will have to undertake a balancing act, between the rights of the creditor seeking permission and the interests of other creditors,[299] taking into account the following:

(i) *"Great importance, or weight"* should normally be given to the proprietary interests of the secured creditor;

(ii) It will normally be sufficient for a grant of leave if *"significant loss"* would be caused to the secured creditor as a result of a refusal. However, if substantial loss would be caused to others if permission is granted, that might outweigh the loss to the secured creditor if permission were to be refused;

(iii) In assessing respective losses, the court will have regard to matters such as:

(a) the financial position of the company;

(b) its ability to pay rent arrears and continuing rent (rent being the issue in that case);

[299] Per Lord Nicholls at pg 542: *"This is not a mechanical exercise but a matter of judgment seeking to give effect to the purpose of the statutory provisions with regards to the parties' interests and the circumstances of the case. The purpose of the power to give permission is to enable the court to relax the prohibition where it would be inequitable for the prohibition to apply."*

(c) the administrator's proposals;

(d) the period for which the administration order has been in force and is expected to remain in force;

(e) the effect on the administration if permission is granted;

(f) the effect on the applicant if permission is refused;

(g) the end result sought to be achieved by the administration;

(h) the prospects of that result being achieved; and

(i) the history of the administration so far.

This is not an exhaustive list.

(iv) The court should consider how probable the suggested consequences are.[300]

8.29 In the case of a mortgagee seeking to enforce his security, *"an important consideration will often be whether the applicant is fully secured. If he is, the delay in enforcement is likely to be less prejudicial to him than in cases where the security is insufficient".*[301] The burden of satisfying the court that permission should be granted rests, at least initially, with the applicant.[302]

---

[300] Pgs 542-4.

[301] Pg 544.

[302] Pg 542.

Company Insolvency – Liquidation

8.30 Liquidation, or "winding up", is governed by IA 1986 Parts IV and V.

8.31 There are three types of liquidation:

(i) Compulsory liquidation – the company is wound-up pursuant to a court order following a petition being presented by the directors, members, creditors or contributors of the company;

(ii) Creditors' Voluntary Liquidation – the members of an insolvent company resolve to wind up the company, following which a meeting of the company's creditors is called pursuant to IA 1986 s.9;

(iii) Members' Voluntary Liquidation – the members of a solvent company resolve to wind up the company, with surplus funds (following satisfaction of any liabilities) distributed amongst the shareholders.

8.32 In the case of compulsory liquidation, creditors of the debtor can apply for a stay of ongoing proceedings against the company under IA 1986 s.126 , which provides:

"(1) At any time after the presentation of a winding-up petition, and before a winding- up order has been made, the company, or any creditor or contributory, may—

(a) Where any action or proceeding against the company is pending in the High Court or Court of Appeal in England and Wales or Northern Ireland, apply to the court in which the action or proceeding is pending for a stay of proceedings therein, and

(b) Where any other action or proceeding is pending against the company, apply to the court having jurisdiction to wind up the company to restrain further proceedingsin the action or proceeding;

and the court to which application is so made may (as the case may be) stay, sist or restrain the proceedings accordingly on such terms as it thinks fit.

(2) In the case of a company registered but not formed under the Companies Act 2006, where the application to stay, sist or restrain is by a creditor, this section extends to actions and proceedings against any contributory of the company."

8.33 After the winding up order has been made, further proceedings are restrained by IA 1986 s.130(2) , which provides:

"(2) When a winding-up order has been made or a provisional liquidator has been appointed, no action or proceeding shall be proceeded with or commenced against the company or its property, except by leave of the court and subject to such terms as the court may impose."

8.34 That prohibition does not, in general, prevent a secured creditor from realising his security.[303]

8.35 In respect of a voluntary liquidation, there is no statutory moratorium on legal process. However, this must be read subject to IA 1986 s.112 which provides for the liquidator to make an application to court in respect of the winding-up, following which the court may exercise any power which could have been exercised in a compulsory winding-up – such as that under s.126. S.112 provides as follows:

---

[303] *Cosco Bulk Carrier Co Ltd v Armada Shipping SA* [2011] EWHC 216 (Ch) at para 49; *Buchler v Talbot* [2004] 2 A.C. 298.

"(1) The liquidator or any contributory or creditor may apply to the court to determine any question arising in the winding up of a company, or to exercise, as respects the enforcing of calls or any other matter, all or any of the powers which the court might exercise if the company were being wound up by the court.

(2) The court, if satisfied that the determination of the question or the required exerciseof power will be just and beneficial, may accede wholly or partially to the application onsuch terms and conditions as it thinks fit, or may make such other order on the application as it thinks just.

(3) A copy of an order made by virtue of this section staying the proceedings in the winding up shall forthwith be forwarded by the company, or otherwise as may be prescribed, to the registrar of companies, who shall enter it in his records relating to thecompany."

8.36 There are no statutory guidelines on how an application under s.126 should be approached, but it is likely that a court will approach any application on a similar basis to an application under s.130(2) IA 1986. The Court is, in effect, given *"a free hand to do what is right and fair according to the circumstances of the case"*.[304]

Company Insolvency – Company Voluntary Arrangements (CVAs)

8.37 CVAs are governed by IA 1986 Part 1. The regime broadly mirrors that for IVAs.

8.38 Part AI of IA 1986 makes detailed provision for the circumstances in which a moratorium may be applied for, by whom, and the procedure to follow. The effects of a moratorium are set out Part A1 Chapter 4. The pertinent provisions, for the

[304] For a useful summary of the applicable principles, see *Armada Shipping* at paras 47-49.

purposes of this Chapter, is s.A21 which provides, so far as is material for present purposes, as follows:

(1) During a moratorium—

(a) a landlord or other person to whom rent is payable may not exercise a right of forfeiture by peaceable re-entry in relation to premises let to the company, except with the permission of the court,

....

(c) no steps may be taken to enforce any security over the company's property except—

(i) steps to enforce a collateral security charge (within the meaning of the Financial Markets and Insolvency (Settlement Finality) Regulations 1999 (S.I. 1999/2979)),

(ii) steps to enforce security created or otherwise arising under a financial collateral arrangement (within the meaning of regulation 3 of the Financial Collateral Arrangements (No. 2) Regulations 2003 (S.I. 2003/ 3226)), or

(iii) steps taken with the permission of the court,

...

(e) no legal process (including legal proceedings, execution, distress or diligence) may be instituted, carried out or continued against the company or its property except—

(i) employment tribunal proceedings or any legal process arising out of such proceedings,

(ii) proceedings, not within sub-paragraph (i), involving a claim between an employer and a worker, or

(iii) a legal process instituted, carried out or continued with the permission of the court.

(2) An application may not be made for permission under subsection (1) for the purposes of enforcing a pre-moratorium debt for which the company has a payment holiday during the moratorium.

(3) An application may not be made for permission under subsection (1)(c), (d) or (e) with a view to obtaining—

(a) the crystallisation of a floating charge, or

(b) the imposition, by virtue of provision in an instrument creating a floating charge, of any restriction on the disposal of any property of the company.

(4) Permission of the court under subsection (1) may be given subject to conditions.

(5) Subsection (1)(c)(iii) is subject to section A23(1)[305].

..."

8.39 If a moratorium is successfully applied for, as with an IVA, it is broad in its scope. In such circumstances, a mortgagee would be unable to commence, or continue, any ongoing proceedings, or to enforce any judgment it may previously have obtained, without the leave of the court.

8.40 As with an IVA, there is no statutory moratorium which automatically applies once the CVA has been approved, and the debtor's creditors may not approve any proposal or modification

---

[305] This relates to security granted by the company during the moratorium period.

which "*affects the right of a secured creditor of the debtor to enforce his security, except with the concurrence of the creditor concerned*".[306] Once a CVA is made, a mortgagee may, therefore rely on the rights and remedies he otherwise enjoyed to enforce his security unless, on a proper construction of the IVA, he consents to those being restricted under its terms.[307]

[306]IA 1986 s.4(3).

[307]*Khan v. Permayer* [2001] B.P.I.R. 95 (CA) at para 19.

CHAPTER NINE

SUSPENSION AND EXECUTION OF POSSESSION ORDERS

9.1 Where the court makes an order for possession of the property it may either make an 'immediate' order[308] (i.e. one requiring possession to be given to the mortgagee by a specified date) or a 'suspended' order[309] in which the obligation to provide possession is postponed or suspended on terms. The court's powers to stay, suspend, or postpone possession are discussed in more detail below.

The Administration of Justice Act 1970 and 1973

9.2 A statutory discretion to stay or suspend execution of a possession order,[310] or to postpone the date for delivery possession, of land including a dwellinghouse is provided for in section 36 of the Administration of Justice Act 1970:

"(1) Where the mortgagee under a mortgage of land which consists of or includes a dwelling-house brings an action in which he claims possession of the mortgaged property, not being an action for foreclosure in which a claim for possession of the mortgaged property is also made, the court may exercise any of the powers conferred on it by

[308]County Court Form CH23.

[309] County Court Form CH24.

[310] The statutory discretion does not apply where the mortgagee obtains possession of the property without obtaining a possession order (i.e. pursuant to his common law right – see para 4.1 above) as s.36 only applies where a mortgagee brings a claim for possession: *Ropaigealach v Barclays Bank Plc* [1993] 3 W.L.R. 17. It also does not apply where the claim is for an order for sale, even though an order for possession would be included in the order made by the court.

subsection (2) below if it appears to the court that in the event of its exercising the power the mortgagor is likely to be able within a reasonable period to pay any sums due under the mortgage or to remedy a default consisting of a breach of any other obligation arising under or by virtue of the mortgage.

(2) The court—

(a) may adjourn the proceedings, or

(b) on giving judgment, or making an order, for delivery of possession of the mortgaged property, or at any time before the execution of such judgment or order, may—

(i) stay or suspend execution of the judgment or order, or

(ii) postpone the date for delivery of possession,

for such period or periods as the court thinks reasonable.

(3) Any such adjournment, stay, suspension or postponement as is referred to in subsection (2) above may be made subject to such conditions with regard to payment by the mortgagor of any sum secured by the mortgage or the remedying of any default as the court thinks fit.

(4) The court may from time to time vary or revoke any condition imposed by virtue of this section. [...]"

9.3 That is augmented by s.8 of the Administration of Justice Act 1973 which provides that:

"(1) Where by a mortgage of land which consists of or includes a dwelling-house, or by any agreement between the mortgagee under such a mortgage and the mortgagor, the mortgagor is entitled or is to be permitted to pay the principal sum secured by instalments or otherwise to defer payment of it in whole or in part, but provision is also made for earlier payment in the event of any default by the mortgagor or of a demand by the mortgagee or otherwise, then for purposes of section 36 of the Administration of Justice Act 1970 (under which a court has power to delay giving a mortgagee possession of the mortgaged property so as to allow the mortgagor a reasonable time to pay any sums due under the mortgage) a court may treat as due under the mortgage on account of the principal sum secured and of interest on it only such amounts as the mortgagor would have expected to be required to pay if there had been no such provision for earlier payment.

(2) A court shall not exercise by virtue of subsection (1) above the powers conferred by section 36 of the Administration of Justice Act 1970 unless it appears to the court not only that the mortgagor is likely to be able within a reasonable period to pay any amounts regarded (in accordance with subsection (1) above) as due on account of the principal sum secured, together with the interest on those amounts, but also that he is likely to be able by the end of that period to pay any further amounts that he would have expected to be required to pay by then on account of that sum and of interest on it if there had been no such provision as is referred to in subsection (1) above for earlier payment.

[...]"

9.4 In effect, AJA 1973 s.8 provides that where a mortgage provides for payments in instalments, but provides for the whole loan to become repayable in the event of default of such payments, the court may exercise its discretion under AJA 1970 s.36 where it appears likely that the mortgagor is likely to be able to pay off those outstanding instalments within a reasonable timescale, rather than needing to be satisfied that the entire mortgage debt could be paid off within a reasonable timescale.[311]

9.5 The conditions in AJA 1970 s.36(1) are strict. If the court is not satisfied as to the matters in s.36(1) then the powers under s.36(2) do not arise for consideration. The court must be satisfied that the mortgagor (or other person entitled to call on the court's discretion) is likely to be able to pay off the outstanding arrears and current instalments within a reasonable period – or that there is likely to be an expeditious sale of the property.[312] The court cannot suspend the possession order, no matter how compelling the mortgagor's circumstances, if there is no prospect of the arrears being paid off within a reasonable period.[313]

9.6 As to what constitutes a 'reasonable period', the starting point will generally be the remaining term of the mortgage.[314] However, in *Cheltenham & Gloucester Building Society v Norgan* [1996] 1 W.L.R. 343, the Court of Appeal identified a number of other factors which are likely to inform that consideration, in

---

[311] AJA 1973 s.8 was introduced in response to *Halifax Building Society v Clark* [1973] Ch 307, in which the court considered there was no likelihood that the defendants would be able to pay off the redemption monies in full within a reasonable time period and that none of the powers in AJA 1970 s.36(2) were therefore available to the court. S.8 will not, however, assist the mortgagor if the loan is not one which permits deferred repayment: *Habib Bank Ltd v Taylor* [1982] 1 W.L.R. 1218.

[312] See, for example, *Royal Trust Co of Canada v Markham* [1995] 1 W.L.R. 1416 per Browne L.J: "*I also agree with Sir John Pennycuick that, for the reasons which he has given, it is not possible to accept Mr. Zucker's submission that in a proper case the court could not stay or suspend an order to enable a property to be sold. I suppose that in all probability this would only be done where there was clear evidence that a sale was going to take place in the near future and that the price would cover all the sums due to the mortgagee for capital and interest. In such circumstances, however, and if the court thought it proper, in my view there would be jurisdiction to make such an order.*"

[313] *Abbey National Mortgages v Bernard* (1996) 71 P. & C.R. 257.

[314] See, for example, *Cheltenham & Gloucester Building Society v Norgan* [1996] 1 W.L.R. 343.

addition to any further factors which may arise in the particular case:

(i) How much can the borrower reasonably afford to pay both now and in the future?

(ii) If the borrower has a temporary difficulty in meeting his obligations, how long is the difficulty likely to last?

(iii) What was the reason for the arrears which have accumulated?

(iv) How much remains of the original term?

(v) What are the relevant contractual terms and what type of mortgage is it (i.e. when is the principal due to be repaid)?

(vi) Is this a case where the court should disregard accelerated possession proceedings (i.e. apply s.8 AJA 1973)?

(vii) Is it reasonable to expect the lender, in the circumstances of the particular case, to recoup the arrears of interest (1) over the whole or the original term, or (2) within a shorter period, or even (3) within a longer period, i.e. by extending the repayment period? Is it reasonable to expect the lender to capitalise the interest or not?

(viii) Are there any reasons affecting the security which should influence the length of the period for payment?[315]

9.7 The power in AJA 1970 s.36 may be exercised even when the mortgage term has expired. In such cases, it appears that the

[315] Evans L.J. at pages 357-8.

court will be considering what is a reasonable period for repayment of the full mortgage debt.[316]

9.8 The question of whether it is "likely" that the mortgagor would be able to pay off the monies due under the mortgage in a reasonable time period will be a question of fact for the court in any given case. It is therefore critical that the mortgagor provide full and frank information as to his finances (including income and expenditure) to enable the court to assess whether that is likely to be the case.[317] The need for such evidence will be even more important in circumstances where the mortgagor has failed to comply with a payment plan under a previous suspension order.[318] The mortgagor may provide evidence by way of witness statement from himself or his solicitor,[319] but must make sure the evidence provided is sufficient: it can be expected, for example, that the court will carefully scrutinise any supporting documents to see if they substantiate claims being made in a statement as to a mortgagor's financial position or expectations.[320] That is particularly likely to be the case if the mortgagor has a poor past payment history, or other history of past conduct which may have a bearing on his ability to meet his obligations if execution of the order is suspended.

9.9 It should be also stressed that the date at which the court will have to be satisfied that the conditions in AJA 1970 s.36(1) are met is the date of the hearing. The court can accept oral evidence from the mortgagor, or documents handed up on the

---

[316] See, for example, *LBI HF v Stanford* [2015] EWHC 3131 (Ch).

[317] *Jameer v Paratus AMC* [2013] H.L.R. 18.

[318] As, for example, in *Jameer*.

[319] *Cheltenham & Gloucester Building Society v Grant* (1994) 26 H.L.R. 703

[320] See, for example, the omissions in the evidence base discussed in *Jameer*

day.[321] It is therefore critical for the mortgagor to attend the hearing at which the issue will be being considered.

9.10 The court may exercise its discretion under AJA 1970 s.36 not only on the application of the mortgagor, but also at the request of a person 'deriving title' from the mortgagor.[322] That does not include a tenant whose tenancy was granted after the mortgage or which is not binding on the mortgagee.[323] A spouse, former spouse, civil partner, former civil partner, co-habitant or former co-habitant may, however, be able to ask the court to exercise that discretion, if they can satisfy the court that the monies due under the mortgage are likely to be paid off within a reasonable time period.[324]

9.11 The court may also exercise its discretion under AJA 1970 s.36 even if the mortgagor is unable to pay the monies due without selling the property. In such cases, the court will need to be satisfied that a sale is likely within a reasonable time frame, and that the proceeds of sale would be sufficient to discharge the mortgage debt.[325] The court is likely to want to see any evidence of marketing activity,[326] the price at which the property is being marketed, and how that price accords with its value.[327] Where there is a dispute as to the value of the property, it would be advisable for the mortgagor to obtain a valuation from a

---

[321] See, for example, *Cheltenham & Gloucester Building Society v Grant* (1994) 26 H.L.R. 703

[322] See the definition of 'mortgagor' in AJA 1970 s.39(1).

[323] See para 6.7 above.

[324] On which, please see the discussion at paras 6.14 – 6.15 above.

[325] The court cannot, for example, exercise its jurisdiction under s.36 where the property is in negative equity: *Cheltenham & Gloucester Building Society v Krausz* (1997) 29 H.L.R. 597.

[326] *National and Provincial Building Society v Lloyd* (1996) 28 H.L.R. 459.

[327] I.e that it is not being marketed at far too high a price – *Royal Trust Bank of Canada v Markham* [1975] 1 W.L.R. 1416.

reputable, and independent, valuer – and not to rely on the evidence of the estate agent marketing the property for sale. Again, the question of what is a 'reasonable period' will depend on all the circumstances; the court may, for example, only allow a very short postponement where there have been previous delays on the part of the mortgagor,[328] although periods of up to a year have been considered in the past.[329]

9.12 Where the court exercises its discretion under AJA 1970 s.36 to adjourn proceedings or postpone the date for delivering up possession of the property, it must do so for a specified period. There is no general power to adjourn or postpone indefinitely.[330] More than one application may be made under s.36, and the court can exercise its discretion to extend, vary or otherwise confer a further period of suspension of execution or postponement of delivery of possession when the discretion under s.36 has already been exercised.[331]

9.13 Where a court suspends an order for possession of the property, it will ordinarily suspend the money judgment on the same terms.

The Consumer Credit Act 1974

9.14 The discretion under AJA 1970 s.36 is not available in respect of regulated agreements. The powers under CCA 1974 Part 9, however, apply to both regulated agreements and, with the exception of s.140B, to regulated mortgage contracts.

9.15 By CCA 1974 s.135, a court may, if it considers it just to do so, make the operation of any order conditional upon the doing of

---

[328] *Bristol & West Building Society v Ellis* (1997) 73 P. & C.R. 158.

[329] See, for example, *National & Provincial Building Society v Lloyd* (1996) 28 H.L.R. 459.

[330] See *Royal Trust Bank of Canada v Markham* [1975] 1 W.L.R. 1416.

[331] *LBI HF v Stanford* [2015] EWHC 3130 (Ch).

specified acts by a party or suspend the operation of the terms of an order either until such time as the court subsequently directs or until the occurrence of a specified act or omission. There is no jurisdictional requirement under CCA 1974 s.135, as there is under AJA 1970 s.36, that the mortgagor be able to clear the arrears within a reasonable period. Whilst an appeal to the court's discretion under AJA 1970 s.36 will be the usual course of action where mortgage arrears are concerned, CCA 1974 s.135 may provide some assistance if the claim for possession is founded on other breaches of the mortgage agreement.

9.16 The court also has the power, under CCA 1974 s.129, to make a 'time order'. A time order may provide for "*one or both of the following as the court considers just*":

(i) the payment by the debtor of any sum owed under a regulated agreement or a security by such instalments, payable at such times, as the court, having regard to the means of the debtor, considers reasonable;

(ii) the remedying by the debtor any breach of a regulated agreement (other than non-payment of money) within such period as the court may specify.

9.17 The mortgagor may make an application for a time order either in his defence or by separate application.[332] Whilst a time order can only be made in respect of 'any sum owed', where a claim for possession is commenced, the time order can be made not only in respect of outstanding arrears but also in respect of future instalments.[333] The court can, in principle, reduce the

[332] In accordance with CPR Part 23 and on form N244.

[333] *Southern and District Finance Plc v Barnes* (1995) 27 HLR 691. Per Leggatt L.J. at pg 697, "*An application for an order of possession is an exercise by the creditor of the right to realise the total indebtedness secured by the charge on the property. As a matter of law as well as of common sense, when a creditor brings a possession action he demands payment of the whole of the sum outstanding under the charge.*"

monthly instalments, with corresponding extension to the term of the agreement.[334] The court may also, if it makes a time order, amend the rate of interest, if it considers it just to do so.[335]

9.18 The court may only make a time order if it is "just" to do so. That will require consideration of all the circumstances of the case, and of the position of the creditor as well as the debtor. The court should consider what instalments would be reasonable, both in timing and amount, by reference to the debtor's means. A time order should normally be made for a specified period of time, and on account of temporary financial difficulties. If the debtor is unlikely to be able to resume repayment of the total debt by at least the amount of the contractual instalments, then a time order should not be made.[336] A time order may be varied or revoked on the application of any person affected by it.[337]

9.19 If the court makes a time order, it should also suspend any possession order it makes so long as the terms of the time order are complied with.[338]

Mortgage Repossessions (Protection of Tenants etc) Act 2010

9.20 As discussed in Chapter 4, where a mortgagee seeks possession of a dwellinghouse which is occupied by an unauthorised tenant, the tenant can apply for a stay of execution of the possession order of up to two months under MRPTA 2010 s.1. Such application can be made by the tenant as a defendant in

---

[334] *Barnes* at pg 198.

[335] Pursuant to CCA 1974 s.136. It cannot do so if it does not make a time order, as an amendment under s.136 must be "in consequence of a term of the order" made by the court under the Act: see *Barnes* at pg 698.

[336] *Barnes* at pg 498.

[337] CCA 1974 s.130(6).

[338] *Barnes* at pg 498.

the proceedings,[339] or following the making of the order but prior to its execution,[340] but the power can be exercised only once.

9.21 The court may order a stay, or suspension, for a period not exceeding two months: it is not an automatic two-month grace period. In determining the period for which the stay or suspension is to be granted, the court must have regard to:

(a) The circumstances of the tenant; and

(b) If there is an outstanding breach by the tenant of a term of the unauthorised tenancy –

(i) the nature of that breach; and

(ii) whether the tenant might reasonably be expected to have avoided breaching that term or to have remedied the breach.

9.22 The court may also make any postponement, stay or suspension conditional on the making of payments to the mortgagee in respect of the occupation of the property.

Execution of the Order

9.23 Where the court makes an 'immediate' order for possession this will usually provide for the defendant to give up possession to the claimant within 28 days. If vacant possession is not provided by the date and time specified in the order, then the mortgagee will need to request a warrant of possession. Such application should be made on form N325 in the County Court, certifying that the property has not been vacated in accordance with the order and providing the prescribed information.[341] A warrant of

339 MRPTA 2010 s.1(2).

340 MRPTA 2010 s.1(4).

341 See CPR r.83.26.

possession will then be issued to the court bailiff (this is an administrative act by court staff), and a notice of eviction will be issued to the defendant, containing a date and time when the eviction is to take place, along with further information.

9.24 Where the court makes a suspended possession order, suspending the execution of the order subject to payments being made by the mortgagor, and there is a default in making those payments, the mortgagee may make a request for a warrant of possession. This should be made on form N325A, certifying the breach, and providing the prescribed information.[342] As with a request made on form N325, a warrant of possession will then be issued to the court bailiff and a notice of eviction will be issued to the defendant, containing a date and time when the eviction is to take place, along with further information.

9.25 There are some cases, however, where the mortgagee will need permission to obtain a warrant of possession. In particular, permission will be required where (i) six years or more have elapsed since the date of judgment or order,[343] or (ii) the mortgagee is relying on non-compliance with a condition of a suspended order, other than the failure to pay money.[344] Any such application will need to be made in accordance with CPR Part 23, on form N244, and be accompanied by evidence.

9.26 Where applying for a warrant of possession of a dwelling-house subject to a mortgage, the claimant must also certify that notice has been given in accordance with the Dwelling Houses (Execution of Possession of Orders by Mortgagees) Regulations 2010.[345]

---

342 CPR r.83.26.

343 CPR r.83.2(3)(a).

344 CPR r.83.2(3).

345 CPR r.83.26(5). The Regulations are discussed in Chapter 6.

9.27 For claims in the High Court, the mortgagee will need to apply for a writ of possession.[346] A writ of possession may include provision for the enforcement of any monies ordered to be paid by the order[347] and where the writ is sought in relation to an order suspended on terms of payment of money by instalments, the mortgagee must certify (i) the amount of money remaining due under the judgment or order and (ii) that the whole or part of any instalment remains unpaid.[348] An application for a writ may be made without notice.[349]

9.28 A mortgagee may not, however, apply for or execute a warrant or writ of possession during a breathing space moratorium or mental health crisis moratorium.[350]

9.29 In respect of either a writ or a warrant of possession, a notice of eviction must be delivered to the premises not less than 14 days before it is executed, and, if not executed in full on the date specified, a further notice of eviction must be delivered to the premises not less than 7 days before the writ or warrant is executed or further executed.[351] The notice must be addressed to all persons against whom the order was made and "any other occupiers", and be in the form prescribed by Practice Direction 83[352] (currently Form N54). The notice must be delivered by:

(i) inserting it through the letter box in a sealed transparent envelope, or, if that is not practicable,

---

[346] CPR r.83.13.

[347] CPR r.83.13(7).

[348] CPR r.83.13(8).

[349] CPR r.83.13(5).

[350] See paras 7.11-12 above.

[351] CPR r.83.8A(2).

[352] CPR r.83.8A(3).

(ii) by attaching a copy to the main door or some other part of the land so that it is clearly visible; or, if that is not practicable

(iii) placing stakes in the land in places where they are clearly visible and attaching to each stake a copy of the notice in a sealed transparent envelope.[353]

9.30 Those requirements are, however, subject to the court's power to dispense with the requirement to deliver a notice of evidence, or to extend or shorten the time by which such notice must be delivered.[354]

9.31 A mortgagor (or other affected party) may apply for a warrant or writ to be suspended, or to be set aside. A writ or warrant for possession may be set aside if the order which it seeks to enforce has been set aside,[355] or the warrant obtained by fraud. A warrant (or writ) may be suspended pursuant to the court's jurisdiction under AJA 1970 s.36. An unauthorised tenant would need to rely on the MRTPA.

---

[353] CPR r.83.8A(4).

[354] CPR r.83.8A(5).

[355] See, for example, *Peabody Donation Fund Governors v Haly* (1986) 19 H.L.R. 145.

MORE BOOKS BY LAW BRIEF PUBLISHING

A selection of our other titles available now:-

'A Practical Guide to Transgender Law' by Robin Moira White & Nicola Newbegin
'Artificial Intelligence – The Practical Legal Issues (2nd Edition)' by John Buyers
'A Practical Guide to Challenging Sham Marriage Allegations in Immigration Law' by Priya Solanki
'A Practical Guide to New Build Conveyancing' by Paul Sams & Rebecca East
'A Practical Guide to Inherited Wealth on Divorce' by Hayley Trim
'A Practical Guide to Shareholder Disputes in Family Businesses' by Ed Weeks
'A Practical Guide to the Law of Forests in Scotland' by Philip Buchan
'A Practical Guide to Health and Medical Cases in Immigration Law' by Rebecca Chapman & Miranda Butler
'A Practical Guide to Bad Character Evidence for Criminal Practitioners by Aparna Rao
'A Practical Guide to Environmental Enforcement' by Christopher Badger & Stuart Jessop
'A Practical Guide to Hoarding and Mental Health for Housing Lawyers' by Rachel Coyle
'A Practical Guide to Psychiatric Claims in Personal Injury – 2nd Edition' by Liam Ryan
'Stephens on Contractual Indemnities' by Richard Stephens
'A Practical Guide to the EU Succession Regulation' by Richard Frimston
'A Practical Guide to Solicitor and Client Costs – 2nd Edition' by Robin Dunne
'Constructive Dismissal – Practice Pointers and Principles' by Benjimin Burgher
'A Practical Guide to Religion and Belief Discrimination Claims in the Workplace' by Kashif Ali
'A Practical Guide to the Law of Medical Treatment Decisions' by Ben Troke

'Fundamental Dishonesty and QOCS in Personal Injury Proceedings: Law and Practice' by Jake Rowley
'A Practical Guide to the Law in Relation to School Exclusions' by Charlotte Hadfield & Alice de Coverley
'A Practical Guide to Divorce for the Silver Separators' by Karin Walker
'The Right to be Forgotten – The Law and Practical Issues' by Melissa Stock
'A Practical Guide to Planning Law and Rights of Way in National Parks, the Broads and AONBs' by James Maurici QC, James Neill et al
'A Practical Guide to Election Law' by Tom Tabori
'A Practical Guide to the Law in Relation to Surrogacy' by Andrew Powell
'A Practical Guide to Claims Arising from Fatal Accidents – 2nd Edition' by James Patience
'A Practical Guide to the Ownership of Employee Inventions – From Entitlement to Compensation' by James Tumbridge & Ashley Roughton
'A Practical Guide to Asbestos Claims' by Jonathan Owen & Gareth McAloon
'A Practical Guide to Stamp Duty Land Tax in England and Northern Ireland' by Suzanne O'Hara
'A Practical Guide to the Law of Farming Partnerships' by Philip Whitcomb
'Covid-19, Homeworking and the Law – The Essential Guide to Employment and GDPR Issues' by Forbes Solicitors
'Covid-19, Force Majeure and Frustration of Contracts – The Essential Guide' by Keith Markham
'Covid-19 and Criminal Law – The Essential Guide' by Ramya Nagesh
'Covid-19 and Family Law in England and Wales – The Essential Guide' by Safda Mahmood
'A Practical Guide to the Law of Unlawful Eviction and Harassment – 2nd Edition' by Stephanie Lovegrove
'Covid-19, Residential Property, Equity Release and Enfranchisement – The Essential Guide' by Paul Sams and Louise Uphill
'Covid-19, Brexit and the Law of Commercial Leases – The Essential Guide' by Mark Shelton
'A Practical Guide to Costs in Personal Injury Claims – 2nd Edition' by Matthew Hoe

‘A Practical Guide to the General Data Protection Regulation (GDPR) – 2nd Edition’ by Keith Markham
‘Ellis on Credit Hire – Sixth Edition’ by Aidan Ellis & Tim Kevan
‘A Practical Guide to Working with Litigants in Person and McKenzie Friends in Family Cases’ by Stuart Barlow
‘Protecting Unregistered Brands: A Practical Guide to the Law of Passing Off’ by Lorna Brazell
‘A Practical Guide to Secondary Liability and Joint Enterprise Post-Jogee’ by Joanne Cecil & James Mehigan
‘A Practical Guide to the Pre-Action RTA Claims Protocol for Personal Injury Lawyers’ by Antonia Ford
‘A Practical Guide to Neighbour Disputes and the Law’ by Alexander Walsh
‘A Practical Guide to Forfeiture of Leases’ by Mark Shelton
‘A Practical Guide to Coercive Control for Legal Practitioners and Victims’ by Rachel Horman
‘A Practical Guide to Rights Over Airspace and Subsoil’ by Daniel Gatty
‘Tackling Disclosure in the Criminal Courts – A Practitioner’s Guide’ by Narita Bahra QC & Don Ramble
‘A Practical Guide to the Law of Driverless Cars – Second Edition’ by Alex Glassbrook, Emma Northey & Scarlett Milligan
‘A Practical Guide to TOLATA Claims’ by Greg Williams
‘A Practical Guide to Elderly Law – 2nd Edition’ by Justin Patten
‘A Practical Guide to the Law of Prescription in Scotland’ by Andrew Foyle
‘A Practical Guide to the Construction and Rectification of Wills and Trust Instruments’ by Edward Hewitt
‘A Practical Guide to the Law of Bullying and Harassment in the Workplace’ by Philip Hyland
‘How to Be a Freelance Solicitor: A Practical Guide to the SRA-Regulated Freelance Solicitor Model’ by Paul Bennett
‘A Practical Guide to Prison Injury Claims’ by Malcolm Johnson
‘A Practical Guide to the Small Claims Track - 2nd Edition’ by Dominic Bright
‘A Practical Guide to Advising Clients at the Police Station’ by Colin Stephen McKeown-Beaumont

'A Practical Guide to Antisocial Behaviour Injunctions' by Iain Wightwick
'Practical Mediation: A Guide for Mediators, Advocates, Advisers, Lawyers, and Students in Civil, Commercial, Business, Property, Workplace, and Employment Cases' by Jonathan Dingle with John Sephton
'The Mini-Pupillage Workbook' by David Boyle
'A Practical Guide to Crofting Law' by Brian Inkster
'A Practical Guide to Spousal Maintenance' by Liz Cowell
'A Practical Guide to the Law of Domain Names and Cybersquatting' by Andrew Clemson
'A Practical Guide to the Law of Gender Pay Gap Reporting' by Harini Iyengar
'A Practical Guide to the Rights of Grandparents in Children Proceedings' by Stuart Barlow
'NHS Whistleblowing and the Law' by Joseph England
'Employment Law and the Gig Economy' by Nigel Mackay & Annie Powell
'A Practical Guide to Noise Induced Hearing Loss (NIHL) Claims' by Andrew Mckie, Ian Skeate, Gareth McAloon
'An Introduction to Beauty Negligence Claims – A Practical Guide for the Personal Injury Practitioner' by Greg Almond
'Intercompany Agreements for Transfer Pricing Compliance' by Paul Sutton
'Zen and the Art of Mediation' by Martin Plowman
'A Practical Guide to the SRA Principles, Individual and Law Firm Codes of Conduct 2019 – What Every Law Firm Needs to Know' by Paul Bennett
'A Practical Guide to Adoption for Family Lawyers' by Graham Pegg
'A Practical Guide to Industrial Disease Claims' by Andrew Mckie & Ian Skeate
'A Practical Guide to Redundancy' by Philip Hyland
'A Practical Guide to Vicarious Liability' by Mariel Irvine
'A Practical Guide to Applications for Landlord's Consent and Variation of Leases' by Mark Shelton
'A Practical Guide to Relief from Sanctions Post-Mitchell and Denton' by Peter Causton
'A Practical Guide to Equity Release for Advisors' by Paul Sams
'A Practical Guide to Financial Services Claims' by Chris Hegarty

'The Law of Houses in Multiple Occupation: A Practical Guide to HMO Proceedings' by Julian Hunt
'Occupiers, Highways and Defective Premises Claims: A Practical Guide Post-Jackson – 2nd Edition' by Andrew Mckie
'A Practical Guide to Financial Ombudsman Service Claims' by Adam Temple & Robert Scrivenor
'A Practical Guide to Advising Schools on Employment Law' by Jonathan Holden
'A Practical Guide to Running Housing Disrepair and Cavity Wall Claims: 2nd Edition' by Andrew Mckie & Ian Skeate
'A Practical Guide to Holiday Sickness Claims – 2nd Edition' by Andrew Mckie & Ian Skeate
'Arguments and Tactics for Personal Injury and Clinical Negligence Claims' by Dorian Williams
'A Practical Guide to Drone Law' by Rufus Ballaster, Andrew Firman, Eleanor Clot
'A Practical Guide to Compliance for Personal Injury Firms Working With Claims Management Companies' by Paul Bennett
'RTA Allegations of Fraud in a Post-Jackson Era: The Handbook – 2nd Edition' by Andrew Mckie
'RTA Personal Injury Claims: A Practical Guide Post-Jackson' by Andrew Mckie
'On Experts: CPR35 for Lawyers and Experts' by David Boyle
'An Introduction to Personal Injury Law' by David Boyle
'A Practical Guide to Subtle Brain Injury Claims' by Pankaj Madan

These books and more are available to order online direct from the publisher at www.lawbriefpublishing.com, where you can also read free sample chapters. For any queries, contact us on 0844 587 2383 or mail@lawbriefpublishing.com.

Our books are also usually in stock at www.amazon.co.uk with free next day delivery for Prime members, and at good legal bookshops such as Wildy & Sons.

We are regularly launching new books in our series of practical day-to-day practitioners' guides. Visit our website and join our free newsletter to be kept informed and to receive special offers, free chapters, etc.

You can also follow us on Twitter at www.twitter.com/lawbriefpub.

www.ingramcontent.com/pod-product-compliance
Lightning Source LLC
LaVergne TN
LVHW022055200926
848481LV00003B/920